CHICKEN, ETC.

D1016199

by
Jean Paré

 Dedication

A tribute to our fine feathered friends.

Cover Photo

1. Polynesian Chicken Salad page 102
2. Chicken Choke Casserole page 21
3. Chicken Noodles Romanoff page 38

China Courtesy Of:
Reed's China And Gift Shop

Napkin Courtesy Of:
Ashbrooks

Window Pottery Courtesy Of:
When Pigs Fly

Slate Courtesy Of:
Global Slate Ltd.

Terra Cotta Pot Courtesy Of:
The Bay

CHICKEN ETC.

Second Printing April 1995

ISBN 1-895455-40-5

Published and Distributed by
Company's Coming Publishing Limited
Box 8037, Station "F"
Edmonton, Alberta, Canada
T6H 4N9

**Published Simultaneously in
Canada and the United States of America**

Printed In Canada

Company's Coming Cookbooks by Jean Paré

COMPANY'S COMING SERIES
English

HARD COVER
- JEAN PARÉ'S FAVORITES
  - Volume One

SOFT COVER
- 150 DELICIOUS SQUARES
- CASSEROLES
- MUFFINS & MORE
- SALADS
- APPETIZERS
- DESSERTS
- SOUPS & SANDWICHES
- HOLIDAY ENTERTAINING
- COOKIES
- VEGETABLES
- MAIN COURSES
- PASTA
- CAKES
- BARBECUES
- DINNERS OF THE WORLD
- LUNCHES
- PIES
- LIGHT RECIPES
- MICROWAVE COOKING
- PRESERVES
- LIGHT CASSEROLES
- CHICKEN, ETC.
- KIDS COOKING (August '95)

PINT SIZE BOOKS
English

SOFT COVER
- FINGER FOOD
- PARTY PLANNING
- BUFFETS
- BAKING DELIGHTS

JEAN PARÉ LIVRES DE CUISINE
French

SOFT COVER
- 150 DÉLICIEUX CARRÉS
- LES CASSEROLES
- MUFFINS ET PLUS
- LES DÎNERS
- LES BARBECUES
- LES TARTES
- DÉLICES DES FÊTES
- RECETTES LÉGÈRES
- LES SALADES
- LA CUISSON AU MICRO-ONDES
- LES PÂTES
- LES CONSERVES
- LES CASSEROLES LÉGÈRES
- POULET, ETC.
- LA CUISINE POUR LES ENFANTS (août '95)

table of Contents

Jean Paré was born and raised during the Great Depression in Irma, a small rural town in eastern Alberta, Canada. She grew up understanding that the combination of family, friends and home cooking is the essence of a good life. Jean learned from her mother, Ruby Elford, to appreciate good cooking and was encouraged by her father, Edward Elford, who praised even her earliest attempts. When she left home she took with her many acquired family recipes, her love of cooking and her intriguing desire to read recipe books like novels!

While raising a family of four, Jean was always busy in her kitchen preparing delicious, tasty treats and savory meals for family and friends of all ages. Her reputation flourished as the mom who would happily feed the neighborhood.

In 1963, when her children had all reached school age, Jean volunteered to cater to the 50th anniversary of the Vermilion School of Agriculture, now Lakeland College. Working out of her home, Jean prepared a dinner for over 1000 people which launched a flourishing catering operation that continued for over eighteen years. During that time she was provided with countless opportunities to test new ideas with immediate feedback – resulting in empty plates and contented customers! Whether preparing cocktail sandwiches for a house party or serving a hot meal for 1500 people, Jean Paré earned a reputation for good food, courteous service and reasonable prices.

"Why don't you write a cookbook?" Time and again, as requests for her recipes mounted, Jean was asked that question. Jean's response was to team up with her son Grant Lovig in the fall of 1980 to form Company's Coming Publishing Limited. April 14, 1981, marked the debut of "150 DELICIOUS SQUARES", the first Company's Coming cookbook in what soon would become Canada's most popular cookbook series. Jean released a new title each year for the first six years. The pace quickened and by 1987 the company had begun publishing two titles each year.

Jean Paré's operation has grown from the early days of working out of a spare bedroom in her home to operating a large and fully equipped test kitchen in Vermilion, Alberta, near the home she and her husband Larry built. Full time staff has grown steadily to include marketing personnel located in major cities across Canada plus selected U.S. markets. Home Office is located in Edmonton, Alberta where distribution, accounting and administration functions are headquartered in the company's own recently constructed 20,000 square foot facility. Company's Coming cookbooks are now distributed throughout Canada and the United States plus numerous overseas markets. Translation of the series to the Spanish and French languages began in 1990. Pint Size Books followed in 1993, offering a smaller, less expensive format focusing on more specialized topics. The recipes continued in the familiar and trusted Company's Coming style.

Jean Paré's approach to cooking has always called for quick and easy recipes using everyday ingredients. Her wonderful collection of time-honored recipes, many of which are family heirlooms, is a welcome addition to any kitchen. That's why we say: "taste the tradition".

Foreword

Chicken, Etc. offers something for everyone. Popular throughout the world as a tasty, nutritious dish, chicken is also economical and versatile. Chicken suits picnic fare, casual or festive entertaining as well as home cooked family meals.

Chicken is low in fat and high in protein. Choose whole birds or parts, either bone-in or boneless. Ground chicken is also available at most grocery stores — a great convenience to have on hand. If you are watching your fat intake or calorie consumption, remove the skin and brown the meat under the broiler or cook with a no-stick cooking spray.

Fresh chicken should be cooked within two days. Frozen chicken, or other smaller poultry, will keep in the freezer up to 9 months. A turkey will keep up to one year. Thaw all poultry in the refrigerator for 3 to 4 hours per pound, (8 to 10 hours per kilogram). Whole chickens will need 12 hours or longer, whereas whole turkeys may take over 48 hours to thaw. For quicker thawing, immerse in cold water about 1 hour per pound (2 hours per kilogram). Before cooking chicken, or other poultry, rinse with cold water and pat dry with a paper towel. If stuffing a whole bird, the cavity should also be rinsed and patted dry, then stuffed just before putting into the oven. This will prevent harmful bacteria from growing. Once a stuffed bird has been roasted, remove all the stuffing immediately. When working with uncooked chicken, it is most important to wash your work surfaces and utensils with hot soapy water after use.

This enticing collection of recipes will tempt new and seasoned cooks. In Chicken, Etc. you will discover such classics as Chicken Wellington and Cock-A-Leekie Soup plus savory Buffalo Wings and Nutty Chicken Scallops. Chicken Pasta Casserole will pique any appetite. You will also find recipes for other types of poultry including turkey, duck, goose and Cornish hen. All the chicken and poultry recipes freeze well, except for stuffed birds, salads, sandwich fillings and stir-fries.

Easy to prepare, reasonably priced and available everywhere — choose chicken!

Jean Paré

CHICKEN SATAY

So tender. Easy and attractive. Terrific appetizer, great for a meal.

Soy sauce	¼ cup	60 mL
Granulated sugar	1 tbsp.	15 mL
Lemon juice, fresh or bottled	1 tsp.	5 mL
Onion powder	¼ tsp.	1 mL
Garlic powder	½ tsp.	2 mL
Ground ginger	½ tsp.	2 mL
Cooking oil	1 tbsp.	15 mL
Boneless chicken breast halves, skin removed, cut in strips or cubes	4	4
Short wooden skewers, soaked in water 30 minutes	34	34
Red peppers, seeded, cut in ¾ inch (2 cm) squares	2	2
Green onions, cut in 1 inch (2.5 cm) lengths	6-8	6-8
Yellow peppers, seeded, cut in ¾ inch (2 cm) squares	2	2
PEANUT SAUCE		
Smooth peanut butter	⅓ cup	75 mL
Water	¾ cup	175 mL
Brown sugar	1 tbsp.	15 mL
Lemon juice, fresh or bottled	1 tbsp.	15 mL
Cooking oil	1 tbsp.	15 mL
Crushed red chili peppers	½ tsp.	2 mL
Garlic powder	¼ tsp.	1 mL
Onion powder	¼ tsp.	1 mL

Stir first 7 ingredients together well in plastic bag.

Add chicken. Squeeze air from bag and seal. Let marinate overnight, or at least several hours, in refrigerator. Turn bag occasionally.

Thread wooden skewers with red pepper, chicken, onion, chicken, yellow pepper. Broil about 2 inches (5 cm) from heat for about 7 minutes, turning once or twice. Chicken will be golden brown. Makes about 34.

Peanut Sauce: Measure all ingredients into saucepan. Heat and stir until it boils. Simmer for 5 minutes until it thickens. Serve as a dip for the satay. Makes about 1 cup (225 mL).

Pictured on page 35.

Start with cooked chicken for these handy little meatballs. So tasty with the mustard dip.

Cream cheese, softened	4 tbsp.	60 mL
Ground cooked chicken	2 cups	450 mL
Chopped chives	2 tbsp.	30 mL
Prepared mustard	1 tsp.	5 mL
Salt	$\frac{1}{2}$ tsp.	2 mL
Pepper	$\frac{1}{4}$ tsp.	1 mL
Liquid smoke	$\frac{3}{4}$ tsp.	4 mL
Milk	$2\frac{1}{2}$ tbsp.	37 mL
Fine dry bread crumbs	2 tbsp.	30 mL
Paprika	$\frac{1}{2}$ tsp.	2 mL
MUSTARD DIP		
Salad dressing (or mayonnaise)	$\frac{1}{2}$ cup	125 mL
Soft honey	2 tsp.	10 mL
Prepared mustard	1 tbsp.	15 mL

Put first 8 ingredients into bowl. Mix well adding a bit more milk if needed to hold shape. Roll into 1 inch (2.5 cm) balls.

Mix bread crumbs with paprika. Coat balls. Chill.

Mustard Dip: Mix salad dressing, honey and mustard in small bowl. Spear smoked balls with wooden pick to dip before eating. Makes $\frac{1}{2}$ cup (125 mL) dip and 32 meatballs.

Pictured on page 17.

He asked for a room and a bath. They gave him a room and said he'd have to take his own bath.

BALI WINGS

Resembles a sweet and sour type. Good.

Chicken drumettes (or whole wings)	4 lbs.	1.8 kg
BALI SAUCE		
Brown sugar, packed	½ cup	125 mL
Granulated sugar	¼ cup	60 mL
Cornstarch	¼ cup	60 mL
Ground ginger	½ tsp.	2 mL
Salt	½ tsp.	2 mL
Pepper	¼ tsp.	1 mL
Water	1 cup	250 mL
White vinegar	½ cup	125 mL
Soy sauce	⅓ cup	75 mL

Arrange drumettes on greased or greased foil-lined baking tray. If using whole wings, discard tips. Cut wings apart at joint. Bake in 350°F (175°C) oven for 30 minutes.

Bali Sauce: Stir first 6 ingredients together well in small saucepan.

Stir in water, vinegar and soy sauce. Heat and stir until it boils and thickens. Brush over drumettes. Continue to bake for 15 to 20 minutes until tender, turning and brushing with sauce at least 2 more times. Makes about 32 drumettes or 48 pieces of whole wings.

Pictured on page 17.

PARMESAN WINGS

Crunchy and cheesy. Delicious.

Plain yogurt	½ cup	125 mL
Lemon juice, fresh or bottled	3 tbsp.	50 mL
Prepared mustard	2 tsp.	10 mL
Prepared horseradish	¼ tsp.	1 mL
Garlic powder	¼ tsp.	1 mL
Ground thyme	¼ tsp.	1 mL
Dry fine bread crumbs	⅓ cup	75 mL
Grated Parmesan cheese	⅔ cup	150 mL
Salt	1 tsp.	5 mL
Chicken drumettes (or whole wings)	2 lbs.	900 g

(continued on next page)

Mix first 6 ingredients in bowl.

Mix bread crumbs, cheese and salt in second bowl.

If using whole wings, discard tips and cut wings apart at joint. Add drumettes to yogurt mixture. Stir to coat. Marinate in refrigerator for 2 to 3 hours or longer. Remove from marinade, drain, roll in cheese mixture and place on greased foil-lined tray. Bake in 350°F (175°C) oven for about 45 minutes until tender. Serve hot. Makes about 16 drumettes or 24 pieces of whole wings.

Pictured on page 17.

STUFFED MUSHROOMS

Tasty little tidbits. Make a few hours ahead, then broil when needed.

Medium mushrooms	24-30	24-30
Butter or hard margarine	3 tbsp.	50 mL
Finely chopped onion	½ cup	125 mL
Finely chopped celery	3 tbsp.	50 mL
Mushroom stems, finely chopped		
Ground cooked chicken	½ cup	125 mL
Dry bread crumbs	¼ cup	60 mL
Sour cream	¼ cup	60 mL
Poultry seasoning	¼ tsp.	1 mL
Chicken bouillon powder	½ tsp.	2 mL
Salt	¼ tsp.	1 mL
Pepper	⅛ tsp.	0.5 mL
Grated Parmesan cheese	2 tbsp.	30 mL

Gently twist stems from mushrooms.

Melt butter in frying pan. Add onion, celery and mushroom stems. Sauté until soft.

Add next 7 ingredients. Stir well. Stuff mushrooms.

Dip tops in cheese. Arrange on baking sheet. Broil on second rack from top for 3 to 5 minutes or bake in 350°F (175°C) oven for 10 to 15 minutes until crusty. Makes 24 to 30.

Pictured on page 17.

BUFFALO WINGS

A fiery color to go with the taste.

Chicken drumettes (or whole wings)	3 lbs.	1.36 kg
Ketchup	⅓ cup	75 mL
White vinegar	2 tbsp.	30 mL
Cooking oil	2 tbsp.	30 mL
Hot pepper sauce	3 tbsp.	50 mL

Arrange drumettes on greased foil-lined baking sheet. If using whole wings, discard tip and cut wings apart at joint.

Mix remaining ingredients in small bowl. Brush drumettes. Bake in 350°F (175°C) oven for 20 minutes. Brush with ketchup mixture again. Bake for 25 minutes more until tender. Serve with celery sticks and Blue Cheese Dip, page 14. Makes about 24 drumettes or 36 pieces of whole wings.

Pictured on page 107.

GLAZED WINGS

A tasty mild zip to these.

Chicken drumettes (or whole wings)	3 lbs.	1.36 kg
Apricot jam	1 cup	250 mL
Cider vinegar	3 tbsp.	50 mL
Soy sauce	2 tsp.	10 mL
Onion powder	¼ tsp.	1 mL
Ground ginger	¼ tsp.	1 mL

Arrange drumettes on greased or greased foil-lined baking tray. If using whole wings, discard tips and cut wings apart at joint. Bake in 350°F (175°C) oven for 30 minutes.

Stir remaining ingredients together in small saucepan. Heat until quite warm so it will spread easier. Brush over drumettes. Continue to cook for 15 to 20 minutes, turning and brushing with sauce 2 or 3 times until tender. Makes about 24 drumettes or 36 pieces of whole wings.

Pictured on page 17.

Good served warm yet also good when cool. Really adds to a tray of appetizers.

CHEESE PASTRY

Butter or hard margarine, softened	½ cup	125 mL
Cream cheese, softened	4 oz.	125 g
All-purpose flour	1 cup	250 mL

FILLING

Finely chopped cooked chicken	½ cup	125 mL
Large egg	1	1
Milk	½ cup	125 mL
Grated Swiss cheese or medium or sharp Cheddar cheese	½ cup	125 mL
Salt	¼ tsp.	1 mL
Onion powder	¼ tsp.	1 mL
Ground thyme	⅛ tsp.	0.5 mL
Cayenne pepper, just a wee pinch		

Cheese Pastry: Cream butter and cream cheese until smooth and light. Add flour. Mix until smooth. Shape into long roll. Mark off into 24 pieces. Cut. Press into small tart tins forming pastry shells.

Filling: Divide chicken among shells, about 1 tsp. (5 mL) each.

Put remaining ingredients into blender. Process until smooth, or beat in mixing bowl. Pour into shells. Bake on bottom shelf in 350°F (175°C) oven for 20 to 25 minutes until set. Makes 24 quiche tarts.

Pictured on page 17.

Paré Pointer

If you tickle a mule he may like it but you will get a far bigger kick out of it.

BOSTON HOT WINGS

Cook wings first, brush with sauce and they are ready to serve. Traditionally served with Blue Cheese Dip and celery sticks.

Chicken drumettes (or whole wings)	3 lbs.	1.36 kg
Butter or hard margarine	3 tbsp.	50 mL
Hot pepper sauce	2 tbsp.	30 mL
White vinegar	2 tsp.	10 mL
Paprika	1/2 tsp.	2 mL
BLUE CHEESE DIP		
Salad dressing (or mayonnaise)	1/2 cup	125 mL
Sour cream	1/2 cup	125 mL
Blue cheese, crumbled, room temperature	1/4 cup	60 mL
Worcestershire sauce	1/2 tsp.	2 mL
Onion powder	1/4 tsp.	1 mL

Arrange drumettes on greased or greased foil-lined tray. If you are using whole wings, discard tips and cut wings apart at joints. Bake in 350°F (175°C) oven for about 45 minutes until tender.

Heat butter, pepper sauce, vinegar and paprika in small saucepan to melt butter. Hold drumettes, 1 at a time with tongs, over saucepan. Brush each with hot mixture. Keep warm. Makes about 24 drumettes or 36 pieces of whole wings.

Pictured on page 17.

Blue Cheese Dip: Beat all ingredients together until smooth. Makes 1 1/3 cups (300 mL).

Pictured on page 107.

CHICKEN FINGERS

These tasty little snacks are baked in the oven rather than deep-fried.

Chicken breasts, halved, skin and bones removed	4	4
Butter or hard margarine	1/2 cup	125 mL
Dry fine bread crumbs	3/4 cup	175 mL
Grated Parmesan cheese	1/4 cup	60 mL
Salt	3/4 tsp.	4 mL
Dried basil	1/4 tsp.	1 mL
Ground thyme	1/4 tsp.	1 mL

(continued on next page)

Cut each chicken breast half into 2 to 3 finger length pieces.

Melt butter in small saucepan.

Combine next 5 ingredients in small bowl. Stir well. Dip each chicken piece into butter then coat with crumb mixture. Place on greased foil-lined baking sheet. Bake in 400°F (205°C) oven for 25 to 30 minutes. Turn at half time. Bake until golden brown and no pink remains in meat. Makes 16 to 24 pieces.

Pictured on page17.

EMPANADAS

Allow extra time to make these little finger foods. An em-pah-NAH-da is worth every nibble.

Butter or hard margarine	1 tbsp.	15 mL
Chopped onion	$\frac{1}{2}$ cup	125 mL
Ground raw chicken	$\frac{1}{2}$ lb.	250 g
All-purpose flour	2 tbsp.	30 mL
Milk	$\frac{1}{2}$ cup	125 mL
Chopped ripe olives	3 tbsp.	50 mL
Raisins, coarsely chopped	$\frac{1}{4}$ cup	60 mL
Worcestershire sauce	1 tsp.	5 mL
Chicken bouillon powder	1 tsp.	5 mL
Hot pepper sauce	$\frac{1}{8}$ tsp.	0.5 mL
Salt	$\frac{1}{8}$ tsp.	0.5 mL
Pastry for 3 or 4 double crust pies		

Heat butter in frying pan. Add onion. Sauté until partially cooked.

Add chicken. Scramble-fry until no pink remains.

Mix in flour. Stir in milk until it boils and thickens. Remove from heat.

Add next 6 ingredients. Stir together.

Roll pastry. Cut into 3 inch (7.5 cm) rounds. Place 1 tsp. (5 mL) chicken mixture in center of each. Moisten half of outside edge with water. Fold over. Press with fork tines to seal. Cut slits in top. Arrange on ungreased baking sheet. Bake in 400°F (205°C) oven for 15 to 20 minutes until browned. Serve hot. Makes $4\frac{1}{2}$ to 5 dozen.

Pictured on page 71.

SWEET AND SOUR DRUMS

Everyone dives in when these are served.

Chicken drumettes (or whole wings)	4 lbs.	1.8 kg
Brown sugar, packed	½ cup	125 mL
All-purpose flour	2 tbsp.	30 mL
Chicken bouillon powder	2 tsp.	10 mL
Garlic powder	¼ tsp.	1 mL
Water	½ cup	125 mL
White vinegar	½ cup	125 mL
Ketchup	¼ cup	60 mL
Soy sauce	2 tbsp.	30 mL

Broil drumettes until browned. If using whole wings discard tip and cut wings apart at joint. Arrange on greased baking tray with sides.

Combine sugar, flour, bouillon powder and garlic powder in small bowl. Mix.

Add water, vinegar, ketchup and soy sauce. Stir together well. Pour over drumettes. Bake in 350°F (175°C) oven for 35 to 45 minutes, basting occasionally, until tender. Makes about 32 drumettes or 48 pieces of whole wings .

Pictured on page 35.

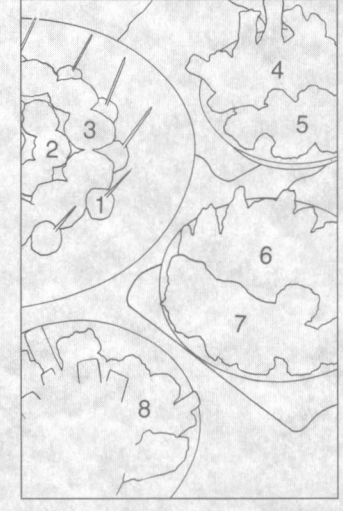

SHERRIED CHICKEN

Rich looking and very tasty.

Hard margarine (butter browns too fast)	2 tbsp.	30 mL
Chicken parts	3 lbs.	1.36 kg
Sliced fresh mushrooms	3 cups	750 mL
All-purpose flour	¼ cup	60 mL
Chicken bouillon powder	1 tbsp.	15 mL
Water	1½ cups	350 mL
Sherry (or alcohol-free sherry)	¼ cup	60 mL
Ground rosemary	¼ tsp.	1 mL

Melt margarine in frying pan. Add chicken. Brown well. Transfer to small roaster.

Add mushrooms to frying pan. You may need to add more margarine. Sauté until soft.

Mix in flour and bouillon powder. Stir in water, sherry and rosemary until it boils and thickens. Pour over chicken. Cover. Bake in 350°F (175°C) oven for about 1 hour until tender. Serves 4 to 6.

CHINESE CHICKEN

This flavorful dish can be prepared early in the day or at the last minute. Just transfer from refrigerator to oven when needed.

Chicken, cut up	3 lbs.	1.36 kg
Soy sauce	⅓ cup	75 mL
Water	2 tbsp.	30 mL
Granulated sugar	¼ cup	60 mL
Ground ginger	½ tsp.	2 mL
Garlic powder	¼ tsp.	1 mL
Onion salt	¼ tsp.	1 mL
Dry mustard powder	¼ tsp.	1 mL
Pepper	⅛ tsp.	0.5 mL

Arrange chicken in single layer in small roaster.

Combine remaining 8 ingredients in small bowl. Stir well. Pour over chicken. Cover. May be refrigerated at this point or placed in 350°F (175°C) oven. Cook for 30 minutes. Allow an extra 20 minutes if refrigerated. Remove cover. Baste. Cook, uncovered, for about 1 hour or until tender. Serves 4 to 6.

Pictured on page 35.

CHICKEN PUFFS

Two recipes in one. The puffs have a smooth golden coating while the nuggets are crumbed and ready for dipping. Serve as an appetizer or main course.

BATTER

All-purpose flour	1 cup	250 mL
Baking powder	2 tsp.	10 mL
Salt	1 tsp.	5 mL
Granulated sugar	1/2 tsp.	2 mL
Large egg	1	1
Cooking oil	2 tbsp.	30 mL
Club soda	1 cup	250 mL
Chicken breasts, halved, skin and bones removed	3	3
Water to moisten chicken		
All-purpose flour	1/2 cup	125 mL
Cooking oil for deep-frying		

Batter: Combine flour, baking powder, salt and sugar in bowl. Stir. Make a well in center.

Beat egg with a fork in small bowl. Mix in cooking oil and club soda. Pour into well. Stir to moisten.

Cut each chicken breast half into 6 to 8 pieces.

Dip chicken into water to moisten. Drain well. Roll in flour. Dip in batter.

Deep-fry in hot 375°F (190°C) cooking oil for 3 to 5 minutes, turning to brown second side. Remove a piece to check now and then to see if it is cooked through. Do not crowd deep-fryer. Remove with slotted spoon to drain on paper towel-lined pan. Put pan in 175°F (80°C) oven to keep warm while finishing cooking. Makes 36 to 48 pieces.

Pictured on page 35.

CHICKEN NUGGETS

Fine dry bread crumbs	1 cup	250 mL
Paprika	2 tsp.	10 mL
Seasoned salt	2 tsp.	10 mL
Salt	1 1/2 tsp.	7 mL
Pepper	1/2 tsp.	2 mL

(continued on next page)

Mix all ingredients in small bowl. After dipping chicken pieces in batter, coat with crumb mixture, then deep-fry. Eat as is or dip in Sweet And Sour Sauce, page 58, or Hot Dipping Sauce page 57. Makes 36 to 48 pieces.

Pictured on page 107.

CHICKEN CHOKE CASSEROLE

A not-so-usual vegetable finds its place.

Hard margarine (butter browns too fast)	2 tbsp.	30 mL
Chicken breasts, halved, skin and bones removed	3 lbs.	1.36 kg
All-purpose flour	1/3 cup	75 mL
Salt, sprinkle		
Pepper, sprinkle		
Canned artichoke hearts, drained and quartered	14 oz.	398 mL
Quartered fresh mushrooms	2 cups	500 mL
All-purpose flour	2 tbsp.	30 mL
Chicken bouillon powder	1½ tsp.	7 mL
Water	1 cup	250 mL
Ketchup	1 tbsp.	15 mL
Sherry (or alcohol-free sherry)	3 tbsp.	50 mL
Ground rosemary	1/4 tsp.	1 mL

Melt margarine in frying pan. Dip damp chicken breast halves in flour. Brown both sides. Sprinkle with salt and pepper. Reduce heat and cook gently turning occasionally until tender. Turn into 3 quart (3 L) casserole.

Tuck artichokes in among chicken pieces.

Place mushrooms in frying pan. Add more margarine if necessary. Sauté until soft.

Mix in flour and bouillon powder with mushrooms. Stir in water, ketchup, sherry and rosemary until it boils and thickens. Pour over chicken. Bake, uncovered, in 350°F (175°C) oven for 30 to 40 minutes until bubbly hot. Serves 4 to 6.

Pictured on cover.

CHICKEN PASTA

This has a topping when cooked as a casserole. It can be served right from the saucepan if time is short. A rich creamy color. Tastes great.

Wide or medium noodles	8 oz.	250 g
Boiling water	3 qts.	3 L
Cooking oil (optional)	1 tbsp.	15 mL
Salt	2 tsp.	10 mL
Butter or hard margarine	5 tbsp.	75 mL
All-purpose flour	5 tbsp.	75 mL
Chicken bouillon powder	1 tbsp.	15 mL
Parsley flakes	1 tsp.	5 mL
Paprika	½ tsp.	2 mL
Salt	¼ tsp.	1 mL
Evaporated skim milk	13½ oz.	385 mL
Milk	1 cup	250 mL
Chopped cooked chicken	2 cups	500 mL
Grated Parmesan cheese	2 tbsp.	30 mL
TOPPING		
Butter or hard margarine	2 tbsp.	30 mL
Dry bread crumbs	½ cup	125 mL
Grated Parmesan cheese	2 tbsp.	30 mL

Cook noodles in boiling water, cooking oil and salt in large uncovered saucepan for 5 to 7 minutes until tender but firm. Drain. Return noodles to pot.

Melt butter in medium saucepan. Mix in flour, bouillon powder, parsley, paprika and salt.

Stir in both milks until it boils and thickens.

Add chicken and cheese. Mix with noodles in pot. Stir. Turn into 3 quart (3 L) casserole.

Topping: Melt butter in small saucepan. Stir in bread crumbs and cheese. Sprinkle over top. Bake, uncovered, in 350°F (175°C) oven for 30 to 40 minutes until heated through and browned. Serves 4 to 6.

Creamy chicken over fine noodles with a crispy-brown cheese topping.

Butter or hard margarine	3 tbsp.	50 mL
Chopped onion	1 cup	250 mL
Sliced fresh mushrooms	2 cups	500 mL
All-purpose flour	3 tbsp.	50 mL
Salt	1/2 tsp.	2 mL
Pepper	1/8 tsp.	0.5 mL
Nutmeg, just a pinch		
Chicken bouillon powder	1 tbsp.	15 mL
Water	2 cups	500 mL
Evaporated skim milk	1 cup	250 mL
Sherry (or alcohol-free sherry)	2 tbsp.	30 mL
Cubed cooked chicken	3 cups	750 mL
Vermicelli, broken up	8 oz.	250 g
Boiling water	3 qts.	3 L
Cooking oil (optional)	1 tbsp.	15 mL
Salt (optional)	1 tbsp.	15 mL
Grated Parmesan cheese	1/2 cup	125 mL

Melt butter in frying pan. Add onion. Sauté for 3 to 4 minutes.

Add mushrooms. Sauté until onion is soft.

Mix in flour, salt, pepper, nutmeg and bouillon powder. Stir in water and milk until it boils and thickens.

Add sherry and chicken to sauce. Heat through.

In uncovered Dutch oven cook vermicelli in boiling water, cooking oil and salt for 4 to 6 minutes until tender but firm. Drain. Add to chicken mixture. Turn into 3 quart (3 L) casserole.

Sprinkle with cheese. Bake, uncovered, in 350°F (175°C) oven for about 20 minutes until browned and hot. Serves 6 to 8.

Paré Pointer

You can tell an elephant is ready to charge when he takes out his Diner's Club card.

POLYNESIAN CHICKEN

Always a tasty combination.

All-purpose flour	⅔ cup	150 mL
Celery salt	1 tsp.	5 mL
Garlic powder	½ tsp.	2 mL
Nutmeg	½ tsp.	2 mL
Paprika	1 tsp.	5 mL
Hard margarine, softened (butter browns too fast)	1 tbsp.	15 mL
Chicken thighs (or mixture of parts)	3 lbs.	1.36 kg
Reserved juice from pineapple		
Soy sauce	¼ cup	60 mL
Brown sugar	2 tbsp.	30 mL
Canned pineapple chunks, drained, cut smaller, juice reserved	14 oz.	398 mL

Mix first 5 ingredients in paper or plastic bag.

Line small roaster with foil. Brush foil with margarine. Coat chicken pieces in bag, a few at a time. Arrange in roaster.

Stir pineapple juice, soy sauce and sugar together in small bowl. Drizzle over chicken. Cover. Bake in 375° (190°C) oven for about 1½ hours until tender.

Scatter pineapple over chicken. Bake, uncovered, about 5 minutes until heated through. Serves 4 to 6.

CHEESY CHILI CASSEROLE

A good, tasty, rich-looking casserole. Just the right chili flavor. This is made one day and cooked the next.

Chicken breasts, halved	2	2
Boiling water to cover		
Corn tortillas	6	6
Condensed cream of chicken soup	10 oz.	284 mL
Finely chopped onion	1 cup	250 mL
Chopped green chilies	4 oz.	114 mL
Milk	½ cup	125 mL
Grated medium Cheddar cheese	1½ cups	350 mL

(continued on next page)

Cook chicken in boiling water for 30 minutes. When cool enough to handle, remove skin and bone. Cut meat bite size. Discard liquid.

Cut tortillas into 1 inch (2.5 cm) strips. Cut each strip into 2 or 3 pieces. Spread in bottom of greased 2 quart (2 L) casserole. Layer chicken over top.

Mix next 4 ingredients and spoon over top.

Sprinkle with cheese. Cover. Refrigerate overnight. Bake, uncovered, in 350°F (175°C) oven for 1 to 1½ hours. Serves 4 to 6.

━━━ CHICKEN AND ASPARAGUS ━━━

It's a natural combination.

Chicken breasts, halved, skin and bones removed	2	2
Hard margarine (butter browns too fast)	1 tbsp.	15 mL
Salt, sprinkle		
Pepper, sprinkle		
Condensed cream of asparagus soup	10 oz.	284 mL
Canned sliced mushrooms, drained	10 oz.	284 mL
Sour cream	½ cup	125 mL
Salad dressing (or mayonnaise)	¼ cup	60 mL
Sherry (or alcohol-free sherry)	2 tbsp.	30 mL
Grated Parmesan cheese	2 tbsp.	30 mL
Frozen asparagus spears	10 oz.	284 g
Grated Parmesan cheese	2 tbsp.	30 mL

Brown chicken well in margarine in frying pan. Sprinkle with salt and pepper. Place in 2 quart (2 L) casserole in single layer.

Stir next 6 ingredients together in bowl. Spoon about ½ sauce over chicken.

Arrange asparagus on top. Cover with remaining sauce.

Sprinkle with remaining cheese. Bake, uncovered, in 350°F (175°C) oven for 1 to 1¼ hours until chicken is tender. Makes 4 servings.

HUNGARIAN CHICKEN

The attractive, zesty color is the result of an abundance of paprika.

Chicken parts	3 lbs.	1.36 kg
All-purpose flour	¼ cup	60 mL
Hard margarine (butter browns too fast)	2 tbsp.	30 mL
Salt, sprinkle		
Pepper, sprinkle		
Hard margarine (butter browns too fast)	2 tbsp.	30 mL
Chopped onion	1½ cups	350 mL
All-purpose flour	2 tbsp.	30 mL
Paprika	1½ tbsp.	25 mL
Chicken bouillon powder	2 tsp.	10 mL
Water	1 cup	250 mL
Ketchup	1 tbsp.	15 mL
Sour cream	1 cup	250 mL

Skin may be removed or left on chicken. Roll damp chicken in flour. Brown in first amount of margarine in frying pan. Sprinkle with salt and pepper. Transfer to small roaster.

Add second amount of margarine and onion to frying pan. Sauté until soft.

Mix in flour, paprika and bouillon powder. Stir in water and ketchup until it boils and thickens a bit. Scrape all bits from bottom. Pour over chicken. Cover. Bake in 350°F (175°C) oven for 1 to 1½ hours until tender. Use tongs to remove chicken to serving dish.

Add sour cream to roaster. Stir. Spoon over chicken or pour into small bowl or gravy boat to serve. A bit of milk may be added to make 2 cups (500 mL). Serves 6 to 8.

Paré Pointer

How do you know that woodpeckers are superstitious? They are always knocking on wood.

CHICKEN TACO CASSEROLE

The choice is yours to use mild or hot enchilada sauce. Crunchy topped.

Chicken parts	3 lbs.	1.36 kg
Water to cover		
Corn chips	¹/₂ × 11 oz.	¹/₂ × 300 g
Canned enchilada sauce	10 oz.	284 mL
Condensed cream of mushroom soup	10 oz.	284 mL
Chopped onion	1¹/₂ cups	375 mL
Garlic salt	¹/₂ tsp.	2 mL
Grated Monterey Jack cheese	1 cup	250 mL
Corn chips	¹/₂ × 11 oz.	¹/₂ × 300 g
Reserved chicken broth	1 cup	250 mL

Put chicken into large saucepan. Cover with water. Bring to a boil, covered. Cook about 45 minutes until tender. Reserve 1 cup (250 mL) broth. When cool enough to handle, remove skin and bones. Cut chicken into bite size pieces. You should have about 3¹/₂ cups (800 mL).

Scatter first amount of corn chips in 9 × 9 inch (22 × 22 cm) pan.

Combine next 4 ingredients in bowl. Add chicken. Stir well. Spoon over corn chips in pan.

Sprinkle with cheese, then remaining corn chips. Pour chicken broth over all. Bake, uncovered, in 350°F (175°C) oven for 45 to 60 minutes. Serves 6 to 8.

Pictured on page 71.

Someone who slaps you on the back usually wants you to cough up something.

CHICKEN IN MOCK WINE

Excellent. Easy to prepare with a gourmet touch.

Red wine vinegar	½ cup	125 mL
Prepared orange juice	½ cup	125 mL
Salt	1 tsp.	5 mL
Pepper	¼ tsp.	1 mL
Garlic powder	¼ tsp.	1 mL
Chicken parts	3 lbs.	1.36 kg
Sliced fresh mushrooms	2 cups	500 mL

Measure first 5 ingredients into bowl that has a tight fitting cover. Stir well.

Add chicken. Cover tightly. Marinate in refrigerator for 4 to 6 hours, shaking bowl every 30 minutes or so. Arrange chicken, skin side down, in small roaster. Reserve marinade. Bake, uncovered, in 375° (190°C) oven for 30 minutes.

Turn chicken skin side up. Add mushrooms around chicken. Pour reserved marinade over top. Cover. Lower heat to 350°F (175°C). Bake for 1 hour more until tender. Baste 2 or 3 times during last hour. Serves 4 to 6.

CHICKEN AND STUFFING

Layer chicken, cheese, mushrooms and stuffing. A great dish.

Chicken parts	3 lbs.	1.36 kg
Poultry seasoning	¼ tsp.	1 mL
Garlic powder	¼ tsp.	1 mL
Salt	½ tsp.	2 mL
Pepper	⅛ tsp.	0.5 mL
Grated mozzarella cheese	1½ cups	350 mL
Sliced fresh mushrooms	2 cups	500 mL
Condensed cream of chicken soup	10 oz.	284 mL
Milk	⅓ cup	75 mL
Dry bread crumbs	¼ cup	60 mL
Package of top of stove stuffing	4¼ oz.	120 g

(continued on next page)

Arrange chicken in small roaster or 9 x 13 inch (22 x 33 cm) pan.

Measure next 4 ingredients in small cup. Stir. Sprinkle over chicken.

Sprinkle cheese over top, then mushrooms.

Mix soup with milk in small bowl. Pour over all.

Sprinkle with bread crumbs. Scatter stuffing directly from package over top. Cover. Bake in 350°F (175°C) oven for 1 hour. Remove cover. Bake about 25 minutes more until tender and browned. Makes 6 servings.

CHICKEN ANGELO

This not-quite-so-common cheese makes this a great company dish.

Large eggs	2	2
Fine dry bread crumbs	1 cup	250 mL
Italian seasoning	1 tsp.	5 mL
Hard margarine (butter browns too fast)	2 tbsp.	30 mL
Chicken breasts, halved, skin and bones removed	4	4
Sliced fresh mushrooms	1 cup	250 mL
Muenster cheese, sliced	¾ lb.	375 g
Sliced fresh mushrooms	1 cup	250 mL
Hot water	1½ cups	375 mL
Chicken bouillon powder	2 tsp.	10 mL

Beat eggs with fork in cereal bowl until smooth.

Stir bread crumbs and Italian seasoning together in a separate bowl.

Melt margarine in frying pan. Dip chicken in egg, coat with crumb mixture and brown both sides well. Arrange in 9 x 13 inch (22 x 33 cm) baking dish.

Sprinkle with first amount of mushrooms. Lay cheese slices over top. Sprinkle with remaining mushrooms.

Mix water with bouillon powder. Pour over all. Bake, uncovered, in 350°F (175°C) oven for 40 to 45 minutes until chicken is tender. Makes 8 servings.

FLAMENCO CHICKEN

A traditional, colorful, tasty dish.

Chicken parts	3 lbs.	1.36 kg
Hard margarine (butter browns too fast)	2 tbsp.	30 mL
Chopped onion	2½ cups	525 mL
Green pepper, seeded and chopped	1	1
Canned tomatoes, broken up	14 oz.	398 mL
Long grain rice, uncooked	1½ cups	350 mL
Water	2 cups	450 mL
Chicken bouillon powder	1 tbsp.	15 mL
Canned mushroom pieces, drained	10 oz.	284 mL
Salt	1 tsp.	5 mL
Pepper	¼ tsp.	1 mL
Garlic powder	¼ tsp.	1 mL
Turmeric or saffron	⅛ tsp.	0.5 mL

Brown chicken in margarine in frying pan. Add more margarine if needed. Transfer to plate.

Sauté onion and green pepper in same pan until soft.

Add all remaining ingredients to onion mixture. Bring to a boil. Pour into small roaster. Arrange chicken over top. Cover. Bake in 350°F (175°C) oven for about 1¼ to 1½ hours until chicken and rice are tender. Serves 4 to 6.

CHICKEN CASSEROLE

Rice ends up as part of the soft gravy. Serves a crowd. Easy to increase. Looks wonderful.

Long grain rice, uncooked	½ cup	125 mL
Condensed cream of celery soup	10 oz.	284 mL
Condensed cream of mushroom soup	10 oz.	284 mL
Condensed cream of chicken soup	10 oz.	284 mL
Water	2 cups	450 mL
Pepper	½ tsp.	2 mL
Chicken parts (or 2 chickens, cut up)	6 lbs.	2.7 kg
Butter or hard margarine, melted	½ cup	125 mL

(continued on next page)

Spread rice in small roaster.

In large bowl, stir all 3 soups, water and pepper together well. Pour over rice.

Brush chicken with melted butter and arrange over soup. Bake, uncovered, in 250°F (120°C) oven for 3 hours until tender. Makes 12 servings.

PINEAPPLE CHICKEN

Sweet, tart and a great flavor.

Hard margarine (butter browns too fast)	**2 tbsp.**	**30 mL**
Chicken parts	**3 lbs.**	**1.36 kg**
Salt, sprinkle		
Pepper, sprinkle		
Juice drained from pineapple		
Water	**1 cup**	**250 mL**
White vinegar	**¼ cup**	**60 mL**
Brown sugar, packed	**¼ cup**	**60 mL**
Soy sauce	**1 tbsp.**	**15 mL**
Salt	**½ tsp.**	**2 mL**
Cornstarch	**1 tbsp.**	**15 mL**
Canned pineapple tidbits, drained, juice reserved	**14 oz.**	**398 mL**
Green pepper, seeded and cut in strips	**1**	**1**

Heat margarine in frying pan. Add chicken. Brown both sides. Sprinkle with salt and pepper. Transfer to small roaster.

Add next 7 ingredients to frying pan. Mix. Heat and stir until it boils and thickens slightly.

Add pineapple and green pepper. Stir. Pour over chicken. Bake, covered, in 350°F (175°C) oven for about 1½ hours until tender. Serves 4 to 6.

FRIED CHICKEN IN CREAM

Rich and wonderful.

Chicken parts	3 lbs.	1.36 kg
All-purpose flour	¼ cup	60 mL
Hard margarine (butter browns too fast)	2 tbsp.	30 mL
Salt, sprinkle		
Pepper, sprinkle		
Sliced onion	1 cup	250 mL
Thinly sliced carrots	1 cup	250 mL
Water	2 cups	500 mL
Salt	½ tsp.	2 mL
Sliced fresh mushrooms	2 cups	500 mL
Whipping cream	1½ cups	350 mL

Coat chicken with flour. Brown well in margarine in frying pan. Sprinkle with salt and pepper. Arrange in small roaster.

Put onion, carrots, water and salt into frying pan. Cover. Simmer slowly until tender crisp. Add to chicken.

Add mushrooms. Pour cream over top. Cover. Bake in 350°F (175°C) oven for about 1½ hours until tender. Serves 4 to 6.

FOILED CHICKEN

Tarragon adds an extra flavor. Easy to prepare and extra easy cleanup.

Boneless chicken breast halves	6	6
Condensed cream of mushroom soup	⅔ cup	150 mL
Sherry (or alcohol-free sherry)	1 tbsp.	15 mL
Chopped green onion	¼ cup	60 mL
Garlic powder	¼ tsp.	1 mL
Ground thyme	¼ tsp.	1 mL
Dried tarragon	¼ tsp.	1 mL
Salt	¼ tsp.	1 mL
Pepper	⅛ tsp.	0.5 mL
Paprika, good sprinkle		

(continued on next page)

Line small roaster with a piece of foil long enough to fold over top of chicken. Place chicken breasts on greased foil.

In small bowl, mix remaining ingredients. Spoon over chicken being sure to put some on each piece. Fold foil over chicken. Bake in 350°F (175°C) oven for about 1½ hours until tender. Makes 6 servings.

CHEESED CHICKEN

Each serving looks so special.

All-purpose flour	⅓ cup	75 mL
Seasoned salt	1 tsp.	5 mL
Pepper	¼ tsp.	1 mL
Paprika	1 tsp.	5 mL
Cooking oil	2 tbsp.	30 mL
Chicken parts	3 lbs.	1.36 kg
Cream cheese, softened	8 oz.	250 g
Milk	1 cup	250 mL
White wine (or alcohol-free wine)	2 tbsp.	30 mL
Chopped onion	1½ cups	375 mL
Canned sliced mushrooms, drained	10 oz.	284 mL
Grated Muenster cheese	½ cup	125 mL

Mix first 4 ingredients in bowl.

Heat cooking oil in frying pan. Roll damp chicken in flour mixture to coat. Brown both sides. Transfer to small roaster.

Beat cream cheese, milk and wine together in small mixing bowl until smooth.

Stir in onion and mushrooms. Pour over chicken. Cover. Cook in 350°F (175°C) oven for 1 to 1½ hours until tender.

Sprinkle with cheese. Cook, uncovered, to melt and brown cheese. Makes 6 servings.

CHICKEN NORMANDY

Layers of onion and apple make a bed for the chicken. Different and good.

Hard margarine (butter browns too fast)	2 tbsp.	30 mL
Chicken parts	3 lbs.	1.36 kg
Salt, sprinkle		
Pepper, sprinkle		
Medium onions, sliced	1-2	1-2
Cooking apples, (McIntosh is good) peeled and sliced	3-4	3-4
Cornstarch	2 tsp.	10 mL
Water	1 cup	250 mL
Salt	¼ tsp.	1 mL

Melt margarine in frying pan. Add chicken. Brown both sides. Sprinkle with salt and pepper.

Put a layer of sliced onions into small roaster. Cover with a layer of sliced apples. Lay chicken over top.

Stir cornstarch, water and salt in frying pan. Loosen all brown bits. Heat and stir until it boils and thickens. Pour over all. Cover. Bake in 350°F (175°C) oven for about 1½ hours until tender. Serves 4 to 6.

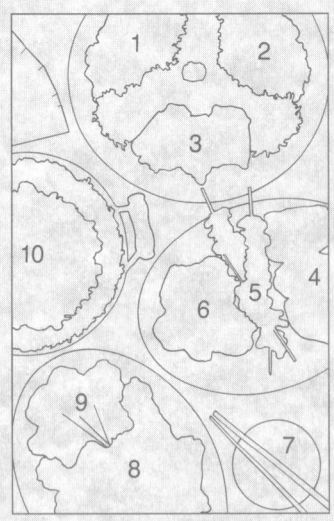

Surprise! A nice greenish color appears as the spinach cooks to the top. An extra good dish.

Frozen chopped spinach, thawed, squeeze-drained	10 oz.	284 g
Boneless chicken breast halves, cut bite size	2	2
Frozen chopped spinach, thawed, squeeze drained	10 oz.	284 g
Boneless chicken breast halves, cut bite size	2	2
Condensed cream of mushroom soup	10 oz.	284 mL
Condensed cream of chicken soup	10 oz.	284 mL
Salad dressing (or mayonnaise)	1/2 cup	125 mL
Curry powder	1 tbsp.	15 mL
Onion powder	1/4 tsp.	1 mL
Garlic powder	1/8 tsp.	0.5 mL
Butter or hard margarine	1 tbsp.	15 mL
Dry bread crumbs	1/4 cup	60 mL
Grated Parmesan cheese	2 tbsp.	30 mL

Layer first 4 ingredients in order given in 2 quart (2 L) casserole.

Combine next 6 ingredients in saucepan. Heat and stir until blended and pourable. Pour over chicken.

Melt butter in small saucepan. Stir in bread crumbs and cheese. Spread over all. Bake, uncovered, in 350°F (175°C) oven for 1 to 1 1/2 hours until chicken is tender. Serves 6.

If you have a rooster and a giraffe you will get awakened on the second floor.

CHICKEN NOODLES ROMANOFF

Creamy white pasta with a browned cheese topping. Very good.

Noodles, medium or broad	8 oz.	250 g
Boiling water	3 qts.	3 L
Cooking oil (optional)	1 tbsp.	15 mL
Salt	2 tsp.	10 mL
Sour cream	1 cup	250 mL
Cottage cheese	1 cup	250 mL
Grated sharp Cheddar cheese	1/2 cup	125 mL
Onion flakes	1 tbsp.	15 mL
Worcestershire sauce	1/2 tsp.	2 mL
Salt	1/2 tsp.	2 mL
Hot pepper sauce	1/4 tsp.	1 mL
Garlic powder	1/4 tsp.	1 mL
Chopped cooked chicken	2 cups	500 mL
Grated sharp Cheddar cheese	1/2 cup	125 mL

In large uncovered saucepan cook noodles in boiling water, cooking oil and salt for 5 to 7 minutes until tender but firm. Drain. Return noodles to saucepan.

Add next 9 ingredients. Stir well. Turn into 3 quart (3 L) casserole.

Sprinkle with last amount of cheese. Bake, uncovered, in 350°F (175°C) oven for 30 to 40 minutes until bubbly hot. Serves 6.

Pictured on cover.

QUICKEST CHICKEN

No pre-browning. Just assemble, put in the oven and do other things while it cooks.

Chicken breasts, halved, skin and bones removed	4	4
Salt, sprinkle		
Pepper, sprinkle		
Canned whole mushrooms, drained	2 × 10 oz.	2 × 284 mL
Condensed cream of mushroom soup	10 oz.	284 mL
Sour cream	1 cup	250 mL
All-purpose flour	1/4 cup	60 mL
Sherry (or alcohol-free sherry)	1/2 cup	125 mL

(continued on next page)

Arrange chicken in 3 quart (3 L) casserole. Sprinkle with salt and pepper. Scatter mushrooms over top.

In bowl stir soup, sour cream and flour together well.

Add sherry. Stir. Pour over top. Bake, uncovered, in 325°F (160°C) oven for about 1½ hours until tender. Makes 8 servings.

TROPICAL DELIGHT

If you want something really different, look no further. Bananas are roasted with the chicken during the last few minutes of cooking. Good.

Skim milk powder	1 cup	250 mL
Granulated sugar	⅔ cup	150 mL
Water	⅔ cup	150 mL
Lemon juice, fresh or bottled	¼ cup	60 mL
Butter or hard margarine	¼ cup	60 mL
Flaked (or medium) coconut	½ cup	125 mL
Ground cardamom	⅛ tsp.	0.5 mL
Green tipped bananas, halved lengthwise, then crosswise	6	6
Corn flake crumbs	3 cups	750 mL
Chicken parts	5 lbs.	2.27 kg
Butter or hard margarine, melted	¾ cup	175 mL

Put first 7 ingredients in blender. Process until smooth. Turn into bowl.

Dip bananas in milk mixture, roll in crumbs and set aside on tray.

Dip chicken in milk mixture, roll in crumbs and arrange in greased 11 x 17 inch (28 x 43 cm) pan or use 2 smaller pans. Drizzle with about ½ cup (125 mL) butter saving rest for bananas. Bake in 350°F (175°C) oven for 1½ hours until tender. Arrange 1 or 2 pieces of banana over each piece of chicken. Drizzle with remaining butter. Bake for 10 to 15 minutes more. Serves 7 to 10.

Pictured on page 53.

CHILI CHICKEN

A mild flavor and a bit creamy. A favorite. It will remind you of lasagne.

Bag of plain tortilla chips	6 oz.	170 g
Lean ground raw chicken	1 lb.	454 g
Chopped onion	1 cup	250 mL
Cooking oil	1 tbsp.	15 mL
Tomato sauce	2 x 7½ oz.	2 x 213 mL
Garlic powder	¼ tsp.	1 mL
Sour cream	1 cup	250 mL
Cottage cheese	1 cup	250 mL
Canned chopped green chilies	4 oz.	114 mL
Grated Monterey Jack cheese	2 cups	500 mL

Pour about ¾ of chips into bowl. Crush. Pour ½ of crushed chips into 3 quart (3 L) casserole.

Scramble-fry chicken and onion in cooking oil until no pink remains in meat and onion is soft. Remove from heat.

Stir tomato sauce and garlic powder into chicken mixture.

Combine sour cream, cottage cheese and green chilies in separate bowl. Stir.

Spread ½ meat mixture over chips in casserole, then ½ sour cream mixture, followed by ½ cheese. Repeat layers. Crush remaining chips and sprinkle over top. Bake, uncovered, for 30 to 35 minutes in 350°F (175°C) oven until heated through. Serves 6.

Paré Pointer

Little love mice kiss mouse to mouse.

TATER TOT CHICKEN

A neat looking dish with flavor to match.

Cooking oil	2 tbsp.	30 mL
Lean ground raw chicken	2 lbs.	900 g
Chopped onion	1½ cups	350 mL
Envelope dry onion soup mix	1 × 1½ oz.	1 × 42 g
Pepper	¼ tsp.	1 mL
Water	½ cup	125 mL
Condensed cream of mushroom soup	10 oz.	284 mL
Frozen tater tots	1 lb.	454 g

Heat cooking oil in frying pan. Add chicken and onion. Sauté until lightly browned. Do in 2 batches to make it easier.

Add next 4 ingredients. Stir well. Turn into 2 quart (2 L) casserole.

Arrange frozen tater tots on top. Bake, uncovered, in 375°F (190°C) oven for about 40 to 45 minutes. Serves 6.

Pictured on page 107.

SIMPLE CHICKEN BAKE

You will find both the chicken and the rice flavorful.

Long grain rice, uncooked	1 cup	250 mL
Chicken parts, skin removed	3 lbs.	1.36 kg
Condensed cream of mushroom soup	10 oz.	284 mL
Water	1⅔ cups	400 mL
Envelope dry onion soup mix	1 × 1½ oz.	1 × 42 g
Paprika	1 tsp.	5 mL

Put rice into 3 quart (3 L) casserole. Lay chicken parts over top.

In medium bowl stir remaining 4 ingredients until mixed. Pour over chicken. Cover. Bake in 325°F (160°C) oven for 1½ to 2 hours until rice and chicken are cooked. Serves 4 to 6.

CHICKEN AND HAM DISH

Delicious. Easy to prepare. Uses leftover chicken and ham.

Butter or hard margarine	4 tbsp.	60 mL
Chopped onion	1½ cups	375 mL
Chopped celery	1 cup	250 mL
Finely chopped green pepper	2 tbsp.	30 mL
All-purpose flour	⅓ cup	75 mL
Salt	½ tsp.	2 mL
Pepper	¼ tsp.	1 mL
Milk	3 cups	750 mL
Condensed cream of mushroom soup	10 oz.	284 mL
Chopped cooked chicken	2 cups	500 mL
Chopped cooked ham	2 cups	500 mL
TOPPING		
Butter or hard margarine	2 tbsp.	30 mL
Grated medium Cheddar cheese	½ cup	125 mL
Dry bread crumbs	½ cup	125 mL

Melt butter in frying pan. Add onion, celery and green pepper. Sauté until soft.

Mix in flour, salt and pepper. Stir in milk until it boils and thickens.

Add soup, chicken and ham. Stir. Turn into 2 quart (2 L) casserole.

Topping: Melt butter in small saucepan. Stir in cheese and bread crumbs. Sprinkle over casserole. Bake, uncovered, in 350°F (175°C) oven for 35 to 40 minutes. Serves 4 to 6.

GO CHICKEN GO

Easy and speedy. No pre-browning of chicken.

Butter or hard margarine	2 tbsp.	30 mL
Hot water	1¼ cups	275 mL
Long grain rice, uncooked	1½ cups	350 mL
Condensed onion soup	10 oz.	284 mL
Condensed cream of mushroom soup	10 oz.	284 mL
Chicken parts	3 lbs.	1.36 kg
Paprika, sprinkle		

(continued on next page)

Stir butter and water together in 9 x 13 inch (22 x 33 cm) pan until butter melts.

Mix in rice and both soups.

Lay chicken over top. Sprinkle with paprika. Cover. Bake in 350°F (175°C) oven for about 2 hours until rice and chicken are cooked. Serves 4 to 6.

SAUCY CHICKEN

A red sauce that adds flavor and color. Nutmeg and cloves may be increased up to four times the amount if desired. Taste as you go.

Margarine (butter browns too fast)	2 tbsp.	30 mL
Chicken parts	3 lbs.	1.36 kg
SAUCE		
Water	½ cup	125 mL
Condensed tomato soup	10 oz.	284 mL
White vinegar	¼ cup	60 mL
Brown sugar, packed	½ cup	125 mL
Nutmeg	¼ tsp.	1 mL
Ground cloves	⅛ tsp.	0.5 mL
Finely chopped onion	½ cup	125 mL

Heat margarine in frying pan. Add chicken a few pieces at a time and brown well on both sides. Skin may be removed before browning if desired. Add more margarine if necessary. Arrange chicken in 3 quart (3 L) casserole.

Sauce: Stir water in frying pan. Simmer and stir to loosen any brown bits. Add remaining ingredients. Simmer slowly for 1 or 2 minutes. Pour over chicken. Bake, uncovered, in 350° (175°C) oven for 45 minutes until tender. Serves 4 to 6.

You are a real optimist if you get treed by a dog and enjoy the scenery.

SPECIAL LEGS

With a sauce that's as good as the legs.

Chicken drumsticks, or thighs or both, skin removed	8	8
Envelope dry onion soup mix	1 × 1½ oz.	1 × 42 g
Brown sugar, packed	½ cup	125 mL
White vinegar	¼ cup	60 mL

Arrange chicken in single layer in casserole or small roaster.

Combine soup mix, sugar and vinegar in small bowl. Spoon over chicken. Cover. Bake in 350°F (175°C) oven for 1 hour until tender. Serve with pan juices poured over top. Serves 4.

APRICOT CHICKEN

This is fast and delicious. It can be prepared without curry but do try it with.

Chicken parts, skin removed	3 lbs.	1.36 kg
Russian salad dressing	½ cup	125 mL
Apricot jam	½ cup	125 mL
Envelope dry onion soup mix (stir before dividing)	½ × 1½ oz.	½ × 42 g
Curry powder	1 tsp.	5 mL

Arrange chicken pieces in small roaster.

Combine next 4 ingredients in bowl. Stir well. Pour over chicken, being sure some is between layers. Cover. Bake in 350°F (175°C) oven for 1¼ to 1½ hours until tender. Serves 4 to 6.

The main reason animals don't dance is that they have two left feet.

HOLIDAY CHICKEN

A dark sauce that is absolutely fantastic. You will need to make extra for sure.

Chicken parts, skin removed	**4 lbs.**	**1.82 kg**
Whole cranberry sauce	**14 oz.**	**398 mL**
Envelope dry onion soup mix	**1 x 1½ oz.**	**1 x 42 g**
Cooking oil	**2 tbsp.**	**30 mL**
Chili sauce	**3 tbsp.**	**50 mL**
Granulated sugar	**⅓ cup**	**75 mL**
White vinegar	**¼ cup**	**60 mL**

Arrange chicken in roaster.

Mix remaining ingredients in bowl. Spoon over chicken being sure to get some on every piece. Cover. Bake in 350°F (175°C) oven for about 1½ hours until tender. Spoon sauce over chicken on warm platter. Serves 6.

PEACH GLAZED CHICKEN

Delicious and dark glazed. Similar to a sweet and sour dish.

Chicken parts	**8**	**8**
Peach jam	**½ cup**	**125 mL**
Ketchup	**¼ cup**	**60 mL**
Soy sauce	**2 tbsp.**	**30 mL**
Dijon mustard	**1 tbsp.**	**15 mL**
Worcestershire sauce	**1 tsp.**	**5 mL**
Salt	**½ tsp.**	**2 mL**
Pepper	**⅛ tsp.**	**0.5 mL**
Garlic powder	**¼ tsp.**	**1 mL**

Arrange chicken on foil-lined baking tray.

Stir remaining ingredients together well in bowl. Spoon over chicken being sure to get some on every piece. Bake in 375° (190°C) oven for 1 to 1¼ hours until tender. Makes 4 servings.

ROMANO CHICKEN

There is a good cheese flavor to this crusty chicken.

Fine cracker crumbs	½ cup	125 mL
Grated Romano cheese	½ cup	125 mL
Garlic powder	¼ tsp.	1 mL
Salt	1 tsp.	5 mL
Pepper	¼ tsp.	1 mL
Chicken parts	3 lbs.	1.36 kg
Milk	½ cup	125 mL

Combine first 5 ingredients in bowl. Stir well.

Dip chicken in milk. Coat with crumb mixture. Arrange skin side up in single layer on greased baking sheet. Bake in 350°F (175°C) oven for 1 to 1¼ hours until tender. Serves 4 to 6.

NUTS ABOUT CHICKEN

Ground pecans or walnuts combine with bread crumbs to make the coating for this. Easy.

Large egg	1	1
Milk	⅓ cup	75 mL
Fine dry bread crumbs	⅓ cup	75 mL
Ground pecans or walnuts	⅓ cup	75 mL
Paprika	1 tsp.	5 mL
Salt	1 tsp.	5 mL
Pepper	¼ tsp.	1 mL
Chicken parts	3 lbs.	1.36 kg
Butter or hard margarine, melted	¼ cup	60 mL

Beat egg lightly. Mix in milk.

In another bowl combine next 5 ingredients. Stir.

Dip chicken into egg mixture and coat with nut mixture. Arrange skin side up in greased pan large enough to hold in single layer.

Drizzle with melted butter. Bake, uncovered, in 350°F (175°C) oven for 1 to 1¼ hours until tender. Serves 4 to 6.

SIMPLE CORN FLAKE CHICKEN

Crunchy and succulent.

Chicken, cut up, or chicken parts	3 lbs.	1.36 kg
Butter or hard margarine	$1/4$ cup	60 mL
Salt	$1/2$ tsp.	2 mL
Pepper	$1/8$ tsp.	0.5 mL
Coarsely crushed corn flakes	1 cup	250 mL

Remove skin or leave on. Pat dry with paper towels.

Melt butter in small saucepan. Mix in salt and pepper.

Brush chicken with butter mixture. Coat with corn flake crumbs. Arrange skin side up on greased baking sheet with sides. Bake in 375°F (190°C) oven for 1 to 1$1/4$ hours until tender. Drizzle with remaining melted butter half way through baking. Serves 4 to 6.

CHICKEN CRUNCH

This is so crusty you will think the skin was left on. Very good.

Fine dry bread crumbs	$2/3$ cup	150 mL
Poultry seasoning	$1/4$ tsp.	1 mL
Parsley flakes	$1/4$ tsp.	1 mL
Salt	$1/4$ tsp.	1 mL
Pepper	$1/16$ tsp.	0.5 mL
Yogurt	1 cup	250 mL
Chicken parts, skin removed	2 lbs.	900 g
Butter or hard margarine, melted	2 tbsp.	30 mL

Mix first 5 ingredients in small bowl.

Put yogurt into bowl. Dip chicken in yogurt to coat, then in crumb mixture. Arrange on greased or greased foil-lined baking pan.

Drizzle with butter. Bake in 400°F (205°C) oven for 1 to 1$1/4$ hours until tender. Serves 3 to 4.

CHICKEN DIABLE

Faintly reminiscent of sweet and sour chicken.

Butter or hard margarine	¼ cup	60 mL
Honey	¼ cup	60 mL
Corn syrup (or honey)	¼ cup	60 mL
Prepared mustard	¼ cup	60 mL
Curry powder	1 tsp.	5 mL
Salt	1 tsp.	5 mL
Chicken, cut up or chicken parts	3 lbs.	1.36 kg

Measure first 6 ingredients into 9 × 13 inch (22 × 33 cm) pan. Melt in oven or over burner. Stir well.

Arrange chicken in single layer in pan, turning each piece so it is completely coated. Bake, uncovered, in 375°F (190°C) oven for about 1½ hours until tender. Serves 4 to 6.

CHICKEN MARENGO

A reddish sauce covers pieces of chicken that cook to perfection.

Grated medium or sharp Cheddar cheese	1 cup	250 mL
Cream cheese, softened	4 oz.	125 g
Chili sauce	½ cup	125 mL
Salt	½ tsp.	2 mL
Pepper	⅛ tsp.	0.5 mL
Boneless chicken breast halves, skin removed	8	8

Combine first 5 ingredients in bowl. Beat until smooth.

Arrange breast halves in pan large enough to hold in single layer. Spread cheese mixture over top. Cover. Bake in 350°F (175°C) oven for about 1½ hours until tender. Makes 8 servings.

Pictured on page 53.

Paré Pointer

Since your hair grows during working hours, you should get time off for a hair cut.

CANTONESE CHICKEN

Cook this right in the marinade. A fantastic glaze.

Chicken parts	**3 lbs.**	**1.36 kg**
Ketchup	**½ cup**	**125 mL**
Soy sauce	**3 tbsp.**	**50 mL**
Liquid honey	**3 tbsp.**	**50 mL**
Lemon juice, fresh or bottled	**2 tbsp.**	**30 mL**
Water	**2 tbsp.**	**30 mL**

Arrange chicken skin side down in small roaster or 9 × 13 inch (22 × 33 cm) pan.

Mix remaining ingredients well. Spoon over chicken. Cover. Marinate in refrigerator for at least 1 hour. Turn chicken over. Cover and marinate at least 1 hour more. Bake, covered, in 375°F (190°C) oven for 30 minutes. Baste chicken. Bake, uncovered, for 30 minutes or more until tender. Serves 4 to 6.

Pictured on page 35.

SESAME CHICKEN

These little seeds cling well while chicken is cooking. Looks attractive.

Fine cracker crumbs	**1 cup**	**250 mL**
Salt	**¾ tsp.**	**4 mL**
Pepper	**¼ tsp.**	**1 mL**
Paprika	**1 tsp.**	**5 mL**
Onion salt	**½ tsp.**	**2 mL**
Sesame seeds, toasted in 350°F (175°C) oven, 5 to 10 minutes	**½ cup**	**125 mL**
Chicken parts or 3 lbs. (1.36 kg) whole chicken, cut up	**3 lbs.**	**1.36 kg**
Milk	**½ cup**	**125 mL**

Stir first 6 ingredients together well in soup bowl.

Dip chicken in milk, coat with dry mixture and arrange skin side up on greased baking sheet with sides. Bake in 375°F (190°C) oven for about 30 minutes. Turn chicken and cook another 30 minutes or until tender. Serves 4 to 6.

Pictured on page 35.

ORANGE CHICKEN

A different, good dish.

All-purpose flour	$\frac{1}{3}$ cup	75 mL
Salt	1 tsp.	5 mL
Pepper	$\frac{1}{4}$ tsp.	1 mL
Paprika	1 tsp.	5 mL
Ground cinnamon	$\frac{1}{8}$ tsp.	0.5 mL
Chicken parts	3 lbs.	1.36 kg
Sliced onion	$\frac{1}{2}$ cup	125 mL
Butter or hard margarine	1 tbsp.	15 mL
Frozen concentrated orange juice, thawed	$\frac{3}{4}$ cup	175 mL

Put first 5 ingredients into paper or plastic bag.

Add chicken, a few pieces at a time. Shake to coat. Arrange on greased foil-lined baking pan. Place skin side up in 450°F (230°C) oven for about 20 minutes to brown. Transfer to small roaster.

Sauté onion in butter in frying pan until soft. Add to chicken.

Drizzle orange juice over chicken. Cover. Bake in 350°F (175°C) oven for about 1½ hours until tender. Baste twice with roaster liquid during cooking. Serves 4 to 6.

CRISPY CHICKEN

A coating flavored with thyme. Crispy like its name.

All-purpose flour	$\frac{3}{4}$ cup	175 mL
Paprika	1 tsp.	5 mL
Salt	1 tsp.	5 mL
Pepper	$\frac{1}{4}$ tsp.	1 mL
Ground thyme	1 tsp.	5 mL
Large egg	1	1
Milk	2 tbsp.	30 mL
Lemon juice, fresh or bottled	2 tsp.	10 mL
Chicken parts	3 lbs.	1.36 kg
Butter or hard margarine, melted	$\frac{1}{4}$ cup	60 mL

(continued on next page)

Measure first 5 ingredients into bowl. Mix.

Beat egg in separate dish. Add milk and lemon juice. Stir.

Dip chicken into flour mixture. Dip into egg mixture and again into flour. Arrange skin side up on greased baking sheet. Let stand 30 minutes.

Drizzle with butter. Bake in 350°F (175°C) oven for 1 to 1¼ hours until tender. Serves 4 to 6.

BAKED CHICKEN PARMESAN

Sensational flavor.

Fine cracker or bread crumbs	½ **cup**	**125 mL**
Grated Parmesan cheese	½ **cup**	**125 mL**
Paprika	¾ **tsp.**	**4 mL**
Salt	¾ **tsp.**	**4 mL**
Pepper	¼ **tsp.**	**1 mL**
Garlic powder	¼ **tsp.**	**1 mL**
Celery salt	¼ **tsp.**	**1 mL**
Onion powder	¼ **tsp.**	**1 mL**
Dried oregano	¼ **tsp.**	**1 mL**
Chicken, cut up or chicken parts	**3 lbs.**	**1.36 kg**
Butter or hard margarine, melted	¼ **cup**	**60 mL**

Combine first 9 ingredients in soup bowl. Stir well.

Brush chicken with melted butter. Coat with crumb mixture in soup bowl. Arrange skin side up in single layer on greased baking sheet with sides. Bake in 350°F (175°C) oven for about 1¼ hours until tender. Serves 4 to 6.

WINGS PARMESAN: Discard wing tips. Cut wings apart at joint. Use instead of chicken parts for a great appetizer.

Girls names should always be used to name hurricanes. Everyone knows there are no himicanes.

BLUE CHICKEN

An amazing flavor. Seasoning is so good, you can't determine what it is.

Hard margarine (butter browns too fast)	2 tbsp.	30 mL
Chicken breasts, halved, skin and bones removed	3	3
Sour cream	1 cup	250 mL
Blue cheese, crumbled (or Roquefort)	4 oz.	125 g
Salt	1 tsp.	5 mL
Pepper	1/8 tsp.	0.5 mL
Garlic powder (or 1 clove, minced)	1/4 tsp.	1 mL
Onion powder	1/4 tsp.	1 mL
Paprika	1/4 tsp.	1 mL

Melt margarine in frying pan. Add chicken. Brown both sides. Transfer into 3 quart (3 L) casserole.

Measure remaining ingredients into same frying pan. Heat and stir to loosen any brown bits. Pour over chicken. Cover. Bake in 350°F (175°C) oven for about 1 hour until tender. Makes 6 servings.

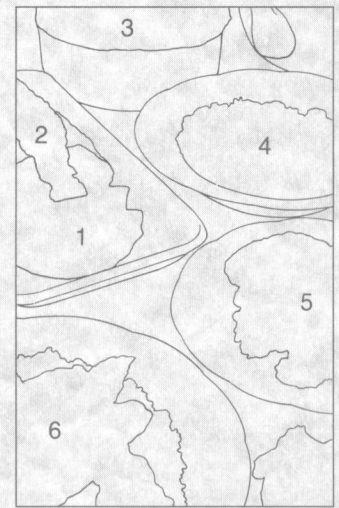

Dishes Courtesy Of:
Zenari's

SIMPLE CHICKEN CRISP

Only three ingredients to this crispy coated chicken.

Chicken parts	3 lbs.	1.36 kg
Italian salad dressing	½ cup	125 mL
Finely crushed corn flakes	1 cup	250 mL

Dip chicken in salad dressing and coat with crumbs. Arrange skin side up in greased baking pan large enough to hold in single layer. Bake without turning in 350°F (175°C) oven for 1 to 1¼ hours until tender. Serves 4 to 6.

MUSHROOM SAUCE

This can be made in a flash using canned mushrooms.

Canned mushroom pieces, drained	10 oz.	284 mL
Butter or hard margarine	3 tbsp.	50 mL
All-purpose flour	¼ cup	60 mL
Parsley flakes	½ tsp.	2 mL
Chicken bouillon powder	2 tsp.	10 mL
Pepper	⅛ tsp.	0.5 mL
Paprika	¼ tsp.	1 mL
Milk	1¾ cups	400 mL

Sauté mushrooms in butter in frying pan until golden brown.

Mix in flour, parsley, bouillon powder, pepper and paprika. Stir in milk until it boils and thickens. Makes 2 cups (500 mL).

TOMATO SAUCE

Ready for dipping or saucing.

Tomato sauce	2 × 7½ oz.	2 × 213 mL
Finely chopped onion	1½ cups	375 mL
Dried oregano	½ tsp.	2 mL
Parsley flakes	½ tsp.	2 mL
Garlic powder	¼ tsp.	1 mL

Put all ingredients into saucepan. Bring to a boil, stirring often. Simmer for about 20 minutes until thickened. Makes 2 cups (450 mL).

Pictured on page 53.

CORN BREAD

Serve as a hot bread or crumble some of it to use in Corn Bread Stuffing, page 64.

Corn meal	1 cup	225 mL
All-purpose flour	1 cup	225 mL
Granulated sugar	3 tbsp.	50 mL
Baking powder	1 tbsp.	15 mL
Salt	$3/4$ tsp.	4 mL
Large egg	1	1
Milk	1 cup	225 mL
Butter or hard margarine, melted	4 tbsp.	60 mL

Measure first 5 ingredients into bowl. Stir.

Beat egg in small bowl. Mix in milk and butter. Stir into dry mixture just until moistened. Turn into greased 9 x 9 inch (22 x 22 cm) pan. Bake in 425°F (220°C) oven for 20 to 25 minutes until browned. Cuts into 16 pieces.

CHICKEN COATING

Could there be anything quicker and handier?

Fine dry bread crumbs	$1/2$ cup	125 mL
All-purpose flour	$1/4$ cup	60 mL
Paprika	1 tbsp.	15 mL
Poultry seasoning	1 tsp.	5 mL
Garlic salt	1 tsp.	5 mL
Salt	1 tsp.	5 mL
Pepper	$1/2$ tsp.	2 mL
Onion salt	$1/2$ tsp.	2 mL

Measure all ingredients into small bowl. Stir thoroughly. To use, moisten chicken parts with water and dip in coating. This is easier to do if coating is put into a plastic bag and each piece of chicken is shaken in it to coat. Arrange chicken on ungreased baking tray. Bake in 400°F (205°C) oven for 40 to 45 minutes until tender. Makes $3/4$ cup (175 mL) coating, enough to coat about $3^1/2$ pounds (1.6 kg).

STUFFED APPLES

A perfect extra to serve with duck or goose.

Cooking apples with peel, (McIntosh is good) halved lengthwise, core removed	3	3
Pitted dried prunes	6	6
Apple juice or water	2 tbsp.	30 mL

Arrange apples cut side up in small baking pan. Place 1 prune in each cavity.

Add juice. Cover. Bake in 350°F (175°C) oven for about 40 minutes until apples are tender. Makes 6.

Pictured on page 89.

CRANBERRY RELISH

Good with anything. Utterly splendid!

Cranberries, fresh or frozen	2 cups	500 mL
Apple, peeled and cored	1	1
Raisins	½ cup	125 mL
Orange, halved and seeded	1	1
Granulated sugar	1½ cups	375 mL
Chopped walnuts or pecans	¼ cup	60 mL

Put cranberries, apple, raisins and ½ orange, including peel, through grinder. Add juice only from second ½ orange.

Stir in sugar and walnuts. Let stand, stirring every few minutes to dissolve sugar. Makes about 2⅔ cups (600 mL).

HOT DIPPING SAUCE

A super easy dip for nuggets, fingers and wings.

Chili sauce	½ cup	125 mL
Worcestershire sauce	½ tsp.	2 mL
Hot pepper sauce	½ tsp.	2 mL
Paprika	¼ tsp.	1 mL

Stir all ingredients together in small bowl. Makes ½ cup (125 mL).

Pictured on page 107.

SWEET AND SOUR SAUCE

Great for dipping nuggets or fingers.

Brown sugar, packed	¼ cup	60 mL
All-purpose flour	1 tbsp.	15 mL
Ketchup	¾ cup	175 mL
Water	⅓ cup	75 mL
White vinegar	2 tbsp.	30 mL
Soy sauce	2 tbsp.	30 mL

Mix sugar and flour in saucepan. Add ketchup, water, vinegar and soy sauce. Heat and stir until it boils and thickens. Makes 1¼ cups (275 mL).

CRANBERRY APPLESAUCE

Double duty. Goes with chicken, goose, duck and any other feathered relatives. Also good with pork.

Medium cooking apples, (McIntosh is good) peeled and sliced	5	5
Cranberries, fresh or frozen	2 cups	500 mL
Brown sugar, packed	1 cup	250 mL
Ground cinnamon	¼ tsp.	1 mL
Ground ginger	⅛ tsp.	0.5 mL

Put all ingredients into saucepan. Heat, stirring often, until it boils. Simmer for 25 minutes. Makes about 2½ cups (575 mL).

BRANDIED CRANBERRIES

This cooks along side of a roasting chicken.

Cranberries, fresh or frozen	2 cups	500 mL
Granulated sugar	1 cup	250 mL
Water	3 tbsp.	50 mL
Brandy flavoring	1 tsp.	5 mL

Put all 4 ingredients into 2 quart (2 L) casserole. Mix well. Cover. Bake in 325° (160°C) oven for 1 hour. Serve hot or cold with any poultry or meat. Makes 1⅓ cups (325 mL).

RICE STUFFING

Easy, moist and delicious.

Long grain rice, uncooked	1½ cups	375 mL
Chopped onion	¾ cup	175 mL
Chopped celery	½ cup	125 mL
Sliced fresh mushrooms	½ cup	125 mL
Salt	1 tsp.	5 mL
Ground thyme	¼ tsp.	1 mL
Ground sage	⅛ tsp.	0.5 mL
Boiling water	3 cups	750 mL
Butter or hard margarine	4 tbsp.	60 mL

Measure first 8 ingredients into medium saucepan. Stir. Bring to a boil. Simmer, covered, for about 15 minutes until rice is tender and moisture is absorbed.

Stir in butter until it melts. Cool for several minutes. Will stuff 4 to 5 Cornish Hens, page 92, or 4 to 5 pound (1.8 to 2.4 kg) chicken. Makes about 5 cups (1.13 L).

PEACH GARNISH

Add a perker-upper to any chicken dish.

Canned peach halves, drained	14 oz.	398 mL
Sour cream	¼ cup	60 mL
Brown sugar	1 tbsp.	15 mL
Rum flavoring	¼ tsp.	1 mL
Brown sugar, 1 tsp. (5 mL) sprinkled over each		

Arrange peach halves cut side up in pie pan. Blot tops with paper towel.

Mix sour cream, first amount of sugar and rum flavoring in small bowl. Spread over peaches.

Sprinkle with remaining sugar. Bake, uncovered, in 350°F (175°C) oven for about 15 minutes. Makes 5 to 6 servings depending on how many halves are in can.

Pictured on page 89.

SHRIMP STUFFING

Not your usual stuffing. Use for Cornish Hens, page 92.

Fine cracker crumbs	⅓ cup	75 mL
Salt	½ tsp.	2 mL
Pepper	⅛ tsp.	0.5 mL
Large shrimp, shelled and deveined	12	12
Boiling water		
Worcestershire sauce	1 tbsp.	15 mL

Mix cracker crumbs, salt and pepper in small bowl.

Cook shrimp in boiling water about 5 minutes until pinkish and curled a bit. Drain. Cool. Pat dry with paper towel.

Brush with Worcestershire sauce and coat with crumb mixture. Put 3 in cavity of each bird. Serves 4.

Pictured on page 89.

POTATO STUFFING

Especially good for ducks and geese.

Butter or hard margarine	6 tbsp.	100 mL
Chopped onion	½ cup	125 mL
Mashed potato	3 cups	700 mL
Dry bread crumbs	3 cups	700 mL
Water	¾ cup	175 mL
Parsley flakes	2 tsp.	10 mL
Ground sage	1½ tsp.	7 mL
Salt	1½ tsp.	7 mL
Pepper	¼ tsp.	1 mL

Melt butter in large saucepan. Add onion. Sauté until soft.

Add remaining ingredients. Mix well. Enough to stuff 8 pound (3.63 kg) goose. Quarter the recipe to stuff 4 pound (1.81 kg) duck. Makes about 9 cups (2 L).

BARBECUE SAUCE

This dark reddish sauce is good. A bit tangy.

Butter or hard margarine	1 tbsp.	15 mL
Chopped onion	½ cup	125 mL
Ketchup	1 cup	250 mL
White vinegar	⅓ cup	75 mL
Water	⅓ cup	75 mL
Brown sugar	3 tbsp.	50 mL
Worcestershire sauce	1 tsp.	5 mL
Prepared mustard	1 tsp.	5 mL

Melt butter in saucepan. Add onion. Sauté until soft.

Add remaining ingredients. Simmer about 20 minutes, stirring occasionally, until mixture thickens. Makes 1¼ cups (275 mL).

CARDAMOM SAUCE

The last touch-up for fried chicken. Different flavor.

Butter or hard margarine	1 tbsp.	15 mL
Finely chopped onion	3 tbsp.	50 mL
All-purpose flour	1 tbsp.	15 mL
Ground cardamom	¼ tsp.	1 mL
Ground ginger	⅛ tsp.	0.5 mL
Pineapple juice	½ cup	125 mL
Soy sauce	1 tbsp.	15 mL

Melt butter in saucepan. Add onion. Sauté until soft.

Mix in flour, cardamom and ginger.

Stir in pineapple juice and soy sauce until it boils and thickens. Spoon over schnitzel or other fried chicken. Makes a scant ½ cup (125 mL).

FAMILY STUFFING

Makes enough for a ten to twelve pound turkey. Halve recipe for a chicken weighing half as much.

Butter or hard margarine	2 tbsp.	30 mL
Chopped onion	1 cup	250 mL
Chopped celery (optional)	¼ cup	60 mL
Dry bread crumbs	6 cups	1.35 L
Chopped fresh parsley	¼ cup	60 mL
Poultry seasoning	2 tsp.	10 mL
Salt	1 tsp.	5 mL
Pepper	¼ tsp.	1 mL
Butter or hard margarine	¼ cup	60 mL
Chicken bouillon powder	1 tsp.	5 mL
Hot water	1½ cups	350 mL

Melt first amount of butter in large Dutch oven. Add onion and celery. Sauté until soft.

Stir in next 5 ingredients.

Mix second amount of butter, bouillon powder and hot water in small bowl until butter melts. Pour over crumb mixture. Toss. When a handful is squeezed, mixture should hold shape. Makes about 11 cups (2.5 L).

Variation: In a hurry? Instead of frying onion and celery, use ¼ cup (60 mL) onion flakes, 1 tbsp. (15 mL) celery flakes and 1 tbsp. (15 mL) parsley flakes.

TOMATO SALSA

Especially for Fajitas, page 69.

Medium tomatoes, diced	2	2
Dried basil	¼ tsp.	1 mL
Dried oregano	¼ tsp.	1 mL
Garlic powder	⅛ tsp.	0.5 mL
Salt	¼ tsp.	1 mL
Pepper	1/16 tsp.	0.5 mL
Cooking oil	1 tsp.	5 mL

Stir all ingredients lightly in bowl. Makes about 1 cup (225 mL).

Pictured on page 71.

A delicious go-with. Serve instead of cranberry sauce.

Cranberries, fresh or frozen	1⅓ cups	300 mL
Raisins	⅓ cup	75 mL
Chopped peach, pear or apple, (fresh or canned) peeled	1 cup	250 mL
Onion flakes	1 tsp.	5 mL
Brown sugar, packed	⅔ cup	150 mL
Prepared orange juice	¼ cup	60 mL
Ground ginger	¼ tsp.	1 mL
Ground allspice	¼ tsp.	1 mL
Salt	¼ tsp.	1 mL

Measure all ingredients into saucepan. Bring to a boil, stirring occasionally. Boil slowly, uncovered, for about 10 minutes until thickened. Cool. Makes 1⅓ cups (300 mL).

Pictured on page 89.

Good flavor to this dense loaf.

Whole wheat flour	3½ cups	800 mL
All-purpose flour	3 cups	675 mL
Baking soda	1 tsp.	5 mL
Salt	1 tsp.	5 mL
Sour milk (see Note)	2½ cups	575 mL

Measure first 4 ingredients in large bowl. Stir. Make a well.

Pour milk into well. Mix into a ball. Knead on lightly floured surface until smooth. Shape into a round loaf. Place in greased round 8 inch (20 cm) casserole. Bake in 350°F (175°C) oven for about 45 minutes. Yield: 1 loaf.

Pictured on page 143.

Note: To sour milk, put 2½ tbsp. (37 mL) white vinegar into measuring cup before adding milk. Let stand 10 minutes.

CORN BREAD STUFFING

Try a not-so-usual stuffing.

Butter or hard margarine	¼ cup	60 mL
Chopped onion	1½ cups	375 mL
Chopped celery	½ cup	125 mL
Large eggs	2	2
Poultry seasoning	1½ tsp.	7 mL
Ground sage	1 tsp.	5 mL
Salt	1½ tsp.	7 mL
Pepper	½ tsp.	2 mL
Chicken bouillon powder	1 tbsp.	15 mL
Water	1 cup	250 mL
Crumbled Corn Bread, page 56	6 cups	1.35 mL
Dry bread cubes (see Note)	7 cups	1.6 L

Melt butter in frying pan. Add onion and celery. Sauté until soft.

In large bowl beat eggs with next 5 ingredients. Add onion mixture.

Stir in water, Corn Bread and bread cubes. Add more water if needed so it will hold shape when a handful is squeezed. Enough for 12 to 14 pound (5.5 to 6.4 kg) turkey. Recipe may be halved or quartered. Makes about 14 cups (3.15 L).

Note: Cut stale bread into cubes. Dry on trays overnight or in oven during the day at lowest temperature.

GUACAMOLE

Use with Fajitas, page 69. Also a good dip for Buffalo Wings, page 12.

Ripe avocados, peeled, pitted and mashed	2	2
Medium tomato, seeds removed, finely diced	1	1
Lemon juice, fresh or bottled	2 tbsp.	30 mL
Minced onion	2 tbsp.	30 mL
Salt	½ tsp.	2 mL

Combine all ingredients in bowl. Stir together. Makes about 1 cup (225 mL).

Pictured on page 71.

Variation: Stir in ½ tsp. (2 mL) chili powder. It will darken slightly but it is very good.

SOUTHERN SAUSAGE STUFFING

Sausage adds that extra flavor. Use for chicken, turkey or goose.

Cooking oil	1 tbsp.	15 mL
Pork sausage meat	1 lb.	454 g
Chopped onion	1 cup	250 mL
Chopped celery	1/3 cup	75 mL
Chopped green pepper	3 tbsp.	50 mL
Large egg	1	1
Poultry seasoning	1 tsp.	5 mL
Chicken bouillon powder	1 tsp.	5 mL
Salt	1/2 tsp.	2 mL
Pepper	1/8 tsp.	0.5 mL
Crumbled Corn Bread, page 56	2 1/2 cups	625 mL
Dry bread crumbs	2 1/2 cups	625 mL

Heat cooking oil in frying pan. Add sausage meat, onion, celery and green pepper. Scramble-fry until no pink remains in meat.

Beat egg in large bowl. Add poultry seasoning, bouillon powder, salt and pepper. Mix. Add sausage mixture.

Stir in Corn Bread and bread crumbs. If too crumbly, a bit of water may be added. Makes 9 cups (2 L) stuffing.

SAUSAGE STUFFING: Omit Corn Bread crumbs. Double amount of bread crumbs. Add water if needed so it will hold its shape when squeezed.

SWEET CABBAGE RELISH

Tasty and different — serve with chicken dishes.

Ripe tomatoes, diced (1 1/4 lbs., 625 g), packed	4 cups	900 mL
Onions, chopped (3/4 lb., 375 g), packed	2 2/3 cups	600 mL
Cabbage, coarsely grated (3/4 lb., 375 g), packed	4 cups	900 mL
Granulated sugar	1 1/4 cups	300 mL
Salt	1/4 tsp.	1 mL
White vinegar	1/2 cup	125 mL
Pickling spice, tied in double layer of cheesecloth	1 1/2 tsp.	7 mL

Put all ingredients into large pot. Bring to a boil, stirring occasionally. Simmer, uncovered, for about 1 1/2 hours. Discard spice bag. Makes 3 2/3 cups (825 mL).

WILD RICE STUFFING

A common stuffing for Cornish Hens, page 92.

Long grain and wild rice mix	6½ oz.	180 g
Butter or hard margarine	2 tbsp.	30 mL
Chopped celery	½ cup	125 mL
Chopped onion	½ cup	125 mL
Canned mushroom pieces, drained	10 oz.	284 mL
Salt	½ tsp.	2 mL
Poultry seasoning	½ tsp.	2 mL

Cook rice according to package directions.

Heat butter in frying pan. Add celery and onion. Sauté until soft.

Add mushrooms, salt and poultry seasoning. Stir. Add to cooked rice. Mix well. Makes enough to stuff 4 hens, about 3½ cups (800 mL).

Pictured on page 89.

SAVORY CHICKEN PIE

Each wedge is a colorful mixture.

Cooking oil	1 tbsp.	15 mL
Ground raw chicken	½ lb.	250 g
Salt	½ tsp.	2 mL
Pepper	¼ tsp.	1 mL
Ground thyme	1/16 tsp.	0.5 mL
Ground sage	1/16 tsp.	0.5 mL
Cayenne pepper	⅛ tsp.	0.5 mL
Garlic powder	¼ tsp.	1 mL
Dried oregano	½ tsp.	2 mL
Large eggs	2	2
Ricotta cheese	1½ cups	375 mL
Grated Parmesan cheese	¾ cup	175 mL
Frozen chopped spinach, thawed, squeezed dry	10 oz.	284 g
Chopped red pepper	¼ cup	60 mL
Pastry, regular or puff, for 2 crust pie		

(continued on next page)

Heat cooking oil in frying pan. Add next 8 ingredients. Scramble-fry until chicken is cooked. Remove from heat.

Combine next 5 ingredients in bowl. Mix with chicken mixture.

Roll pastry and line 9 inch (22 cm) pie plate. Pour chicken mixture into shell. Roll top crust. Dampen edges. Cover with top crust. Trim and crimp to seal. Cut slits in top. Bake on bottom shelf in 400°F (205°C) oven for about 45 minutes until browned. Makes 8 servings.

CHICKEN BURRITOS

Serve these wonderful burritos with sour cream for dipping. Make lots.

Cooking oil	2 tbsp.	30 mL
Chicken breasts, halved, skin and bones removed, cut in strips	2	2
Green pepper, seeded and chopped	1	1
Red pepper, seeded and chopped	1	1
Green onions, sliced	4	4
Very finely chopped canned jalapeño pepper	1 tbsp.	15 mL
Ground coriander	1 tbsp.	15 mL
Garlic powder (or 1 clove, minced)	1/4 tsp.	1 mL
Flour tortillas	8	8
Medium tomatoes, seeded and diced	2	2
Grated medium Cheddar cheese	1 cup	250 mL
Grated medium Cheddar cheese	3/4 cup	175 mL

Heat cooking oil in frying pan. Add next 7 ingredients. Stir-fry until no pink remains in chicken and peppers soften.

On each tortilla, spoon 1/8 mixture in a row off center. Divide tomatoes and first amount of cheese evenly on top of chicken mixture. Roll tortillas as for jelly roll, tucking sides in as you roll. Lay seam side down on 9 x 13 inch (22 x 33 cm) pan.

Sprinkle with remaining cheese. Cover. Heat in 350° (175°C) oven for 25 to 40 minutes to heat through. Serves 4.

Pictured on page 71.

CHICKEN ENCHILADAS

This begins with a filling and ends with a pan full of wonderful enchiladas.

Cooking oil	2 tbsp.	30 mL
Chicken breasts, halved, skin and bones removed, diced	4	4
Chopped onion	1 cup	250 mL
Garlic clove, minced (or ¼ tsp., 1 mL, garlic powder)	1	1
Canned sliced mushrooms, drained	10 oz.	284 mL
Canned chopped green chilies, drained	4 oz.	114 mL
Sour cream	1 cup	250 mL
Chili powder	1 tsp.	5 mL
Ground cumin	1 tsp.	5 mL
Salt	½ tsp.	2 mL
Pepper	¼ tsp.	1 mL
Cooking oil	½ cup	125 mL
Corn tortillas	16	16
Grated medium Cheddar cheese or Monterey Jack	2 cups	500 mL
TOPPING		
Sour cream	2 cups	500 mL
Grated medium Cheddar cheese or Monterey Jack	2 cups	500 mL

Heat cooking oil in frying pan. Add chicken, onion and garlic. Stir-fry until no pink remains in meat.

Stir next 7 ingredients together well in bowl. Add chicken mixture.

Heat second amount of cooking oil in frying pan. Using tongs, dip each tortilla into cooking oil to soften for 3 to 5 seconds per side. Add more cooking oil if needed. Drain on paper towels. Place scant ¼ cup (60 mL) chicken mixture in center of each tortilla.

Add 2 tbsp. (30 mL) cheese. Roll tortilla tightly around filling. Arrange seam side down in 1 or 2 greased pans. Bake, uncovered, in 350°F (175°C) oven for 15 minutes until hot.

Topping: Spread sour cream over top. Sprinkle with cheese. Return to oven for about 5 minutes. Makes 16.

Pictured on page 71.

For a real fun meal, try fa-HEE-tahs. Serve with or without peppers.

Cooking oil	1 tbsp.	15 mL
Chicken breast halves, skin and bones removed, sliced in long thin strips	4	4
Spanish onion, sliced in rings	1	1
Green pepper, seeded and cut in strips (see Note)	1	1
Red pepper, seeded and cut in strips (see Note)	1	1
Salt, sprinkle		
Pepper, sprinkle		
Lemon juice, fresh or bottled	1 tbsp.	15 mL
Flour tortillas, 7 inch (18 cm), heated in covered bowl	8-10	8-10
Grated medium or sharp Cheddar cheese	1 cup	250 mL
Sour cream	1 cup	250 mL
Tomato Salsa, page 62	1 cup	250 mL
Guacamole, page 64	1 cup	250 mL

Heat cooking oil in frying pan. Add chicken. Stir-fry until cooked. Turn into bowl.

To same frying pan, add onion, green and red peppers and more cooking oil if needed. Sauté until browned. Spread on warm platter.

Return chicken to pan to heat. Sprinkle with salt and pepper. Drizzle with lemon juice. Heat quickly. Place over onion mixture.

To prepare for eating, lay 1 tortilla on plate. Place some onion mixture down center, then a few chicken strips on top. Garnish with cheese, sour cream, Salsa and Guacamole. Roll. Fold up and hold one end while you bite from the other end. Makes 8 to 10 fajitas.

Note: To make without peppers, use 2 onions.

Pictured on page 71.

Little boys who never tell the truth become weather men when they grow up.

CHICKEN QUICHE

Lots of chicken in this.

Chopped cooked chicken	2 cups	500 mL
Unbaked 9 inch (22 cm) pie shell	1	1
Dry bread crumbs	1/4 cup	60 mL
Onion flakes	1 tbsp.	15 mL
Parsley flakes	1/2 tsp.	2 mL
Poultry seasoning	1/2 tsp.	2 mL
Celery flakes	1/4 tsp.	1 mL
Salt	1/2 tsp.	2 mL
Large eggs	2	2
All-purpose flour	3 tbsp.	50 mL
Milk	1 1/4 cups	300 mL

Scatter chicken in pie shell.

Mix next 6 ingredients in small bowl. Sprinkle over chicken.

Beat eggs until frothy. Beat in flour. Add milk. Stir. Pour over top. Bake on bottom shelf in 350°F (175°C) oven for about 40 to 50 minutes until set. Makes 6 servings as a main course and 10 servings as an appetizer.

1. Chicken Enchiladas page 68
2. Chicken Taco Casserole page 27
3. Trendy Tacos page 112
4. Guacamole page 64
5. Fajitas page 69
6. Breakfast Burrito page 110
7. Chicken Burrito page 67
8. Burritos page 77
9. Empanadas page 15
10. Tomato Salsa page 62

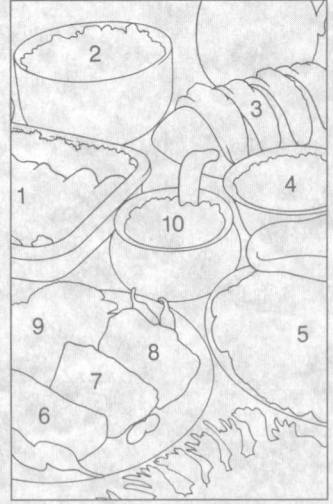

Pastry is lined with a mushroom-onion mixture and ham. Fancy.

Large chicken breasts, halved, skin and bones removed	3	3
Hard margarine (butter browns too fast)	1 tbsp.	15 mL
Salt, sprinkle		
Pepper, sprinkle		
Finely chopped onion	$\frac{3}{4}$ cup	175 mL
Finely chopped fresh mushrooms	$\frac{3}{4}$ cup	175 mL
Canned ham flakes, drained and mashed	$6\frac{1}{2}$ oz.	184 g
Salad dressing (or mayonnaise)	1 tbsp.	15 mL
Frozen puff pastry, thawed	14 oz.	397 g
Large egg, beaten (optional)	1	1

Cook chicken in margarine in frying pan, browning both sides. Sprinkle with salt and pepper. Remove to plate. Cool well.

Sauté onion and mushrooms in same frying pan until soft, adding more margarine if needed. Cool.

Mix ham and salad dressing together.

Cut pastry into 6 equal pieces. For 1 Wellington, roll pastry and cut 2 pieces about 1 inch (2.5 cm) larger than chicken breast half. Spread $\frac{1}{6}$ ham mixture on 1 piece keeping it in 1 inch (2.5 cm) from edge. Lay chicken on top. Spread $\frac{1}{6}$ onion mixture over chicken. Cover with second piece of pastry. Dampen edges with water. Pinch to seal. Cut slits in top. Repeat. Arrange on baking sheet.

Brush with egg if desired. Bake in 400°F (205°C) oven for about 20 to 25 minutes until browned. Makes 6 individual Wellingtons.

Pictured on page 89.

Paré Pointer

After teaching chemistry for a few years, he found nitrates were cheaper than day rates.

CHICKEN LASAGNE

Always a favorite.

Lasagne noodles	10	10
Boiling water	4 qts.	4 L
Cooking oil (optional)	1 tbsp.	15 mL
Salt	1 tbsp.	15 mL
CHICKEN SAUCE		
Butter or hard margarine	2 tbsp.	30 mL
Finely chopped onion	1 cup	250 mL
Ground raw chicken, (or chopped cooked chicken)	1¼ lbs.	570 g
Condensed chicken broth	10 oz.	284 mL
Canned sliced mushrooms, drained	10 oz.	284 mL
Canned tomatoes, broken up	14 oz.	398 mL
Tomato paste	5½ oz.	156 mL
Dried basil	1 tsp.	5 mL
Garlic powder	¼ tsp.	1 mL
Dried oregano	½ tsp.	2 mL
Salt	¾ tsp.	4 mL
Pepper	¼ tsp.	1 mL
Large egg	1	1
Cottage cheese	1 cup	250 mL
Grated Parmesan cheese	¼ cup	60 mL
Grated Mozzarella cheese	2 cups	500 mL
Grated Parmesan cheese	¼ cup	60 mL

Cook noodles in boiling water, cooking oil and salt in uncovered Dutch oven for 14 to 16 minutes until tender but firm. Drain.

Chicken Sauce: Melt butter in large pot. Add onion and chicken. Scramble-fry until browned.

Add next 9 ingredients. Stir. Bring to a boil. Simmer for about 20 minutes.

Mix egg, cottage cheese and first amount of Parmesan cheese to small bowl.

(continued on next page)

To assemble, layer in greased 9 x 13 inch (22 x 33 cm) pan as follows:

1. Layer of noodles
2. ½ chicken sauce
3. All of cottage cheese mixture
4. Layer of noodles
5. ½ chicken sauce
6. Mozzarella cheese
7. Parmesan cheese (second amount)

Cover with greased foil. Bake in 350°F (175°C) oven for about 35 minutes. Remove cover. Bake about 10 minutes more to brown cheese lightly. Let stand 10 minutes before cutting. Serves 8.

CHICKEN MUSHROOM PIE

Also includes bacon. Different and delicious.

Bacon slices, diced	6	6
Chopped onion	1¼ cups	300 mL
Canned whole mushrooms, drained	10 oz.	284 mL
Diced cooked chicken	3 cups	675 mL
Parsley flakes	1 tsp.	5 mL
All-purpose flour	1 tbsp.	15 mL
Salt	½ tsp.	2 mL
Pepper	¼ tsp.	1 mL
Hot water	1 cup	250 mL
Vegetable bouillon powder	1 tsp.	5 mL
Chicken bouillon powder	1 tsp.	5 mL
Frozen puff pastry, thawed	½ x 14 oz.	½ x 397 g

Stir-fry bacon and onion until onion is soft. Turn into large bowl.

Add next 6 ingredients. Stir together well.

Mix water and bouillon powders together. Pour over contents in bowl. Stir well. Turn into 3 quart (3 L) casserole.

Roll pastry about 1 inch (2.5 cm) wider than casserole dish. Fit over top of food allowing it to come up sides. Cut slits in top. Use extra bits of pastry to put cutouts on top. Bake in 400°F (205°C) oven for 35 to 40 minutes until browned. Makes 6 servings.

Pictured on page 53.

CHICKEN SHORTCAKE

Showy and as good as it is different.

BISCUIT LAYERS

All-purpose flour	4 cups	900 mL
Baking powder	4 tsp.	20 mL
Salt	2 tsp.	10 mL
Cold butter or hard margarine	¾ cup	175 mL
Milk	1½ cups	350 mL
Butter or hard margarine, softened	1 tbsp.	15 mL

FILLING

Butter or hard margarine	2 tbsp.	30 mL
Chopped onion	¾ cup	175 mL
Finely chopped celery	⅓ cup	75 mL
Grated carrot	1 cup	250 mL
All-purpose flour	⅓ cup	75 mL
Beef bouillon powder	1 tbsp.	15 mL
Milk (part cream adds extra richness)	3¼ cups	725 mL
Chopped cooked chicken, dark and white meat	2½ cups	600 mL
Salt	½ tsp.	2 mL
Pepper	⅛ tsp.	0.5 mL

Biscuit Layers: Stir flour, baking powder and salt in bowl. Cut in butter until mixture is crumbly.

Add milk. Stir to form a soft ball. Turn out onto lightly floured surface. Divide dough into 2 equal parts. Roll each part into an 8 x 8 inch (20 x 20 cm) square.

Place 1 square on ungreased baking sheet. Spread with butter. Lay second square over first square. Bake as one unit in 400°F (205°C) oven for about 20 minutes.

Filling: Melt butter in frying pan. Add onion, celery and carrot. Sauté until soft.

Mix in flour and bouillon powder. Stir in milk until it boils and thickens.

Add remaining ingredients. Stir. Heat through. Carefully split shortcake into layers. Spread about ⅔ filling over bottom layer. Cover with other layer. Spoon remaining ⅓ filling over top. Cut into 6 pieces to serve 6.

A big, chubby burrito with beans, cheese, vegetables and chicken.

Chopped onion	½ cup	125 mL
Ripe tomatoes, scalded, peeled and chopped	2	2
Canned whole jalapeño pepper, finely chopped	1 tbsp.	15 mL
Ketchup	1 tbsp.	15 mL
Lemon juice, fresh or bottled	1 tbsp.	15 mL
Granulated sugar	1 tsp.	5 mL
Diced cooked chicken	1½ cups	375 mL
Flour tortillas, 8 inch (20 cm)	6	6
Canned refried beans (see Variation)	1 cup	250 mL
Grated Monterey Jack cheese	1 cup	250 mL
Grated Monterey Jack cheese	1 cup	250 mL
Sour cream	½ cup	125 mL

Put first 6 ingredients into saucepan. Heat, stirring often until it boils. Simmer, uncovered, for about 15 minutes until onion is cooked and sauce thickens.

Stir in chicken. Heat through.

On each tortilla, put mashed beans down center. Spoon chicken mixture over beans followed by first amount of cheese. Roll up, tucking in sides as you go in envelope fashion. Place seam side down in baking dish.

Sprinkle with second amount of cheese. Spoon sour cream across center. Bake, uncovered, in 350°F (175°C) oven for 30 to 45 minutes. Makes 6 servings.

Pictured on page 71.

Variation: Omit refried beans. Discard pork from canned 8 oz. (227 mL) pork and beans and mash beans. Canned kidney beans, drained and mashed may also be used.

Paré Pointer

She thinks a net profit is what a fisherman earns.

PASTA CHICKEN CAKE

Allow extra time to make this. The second time will be quicker. An extraordinary show piece. Two noodle layers with a chicken filling.

FILLING

Butter or hard margarine	1 tbsp.	15 mL
Finely chopped onion	1 cup	250 mL
Dried oregano	1/2 tsp.	2 mL
Ground thyme	1/2 tsp.	2 mL
Grated medium or sharp Cheddar cheese	1 cup	250 mL
Chopped cooked chicken	2 cups	500 mL
Salad dressing (or mayonnaise)	3 tbsp.	50 mL
Ketchup	1 tbsp.	15 mL
Salt	1/2 tsp.	2 mL
Pepper	1/16 tsp.	0.5 mL
Evaporated milk	1/2 cup	125 mL

PASTA

Spaghetti	3/4 lb.	375 g
Boiling water	3 qts.	3 L
Cooking oil (optional)	1 tbsp.	15 mL
Salt	2 tsp.	10 mL

SAUCE

Butter or hard margarine	3 tbsp.	50 mL
Finely chopped onion	3/4 cup	175 mL
All-purpose flour	3 tbsp.	50 mL
Chicken bouillon powder	2 tsp.	10 mL
Salt	1/2 tsp.	2 mL
Pepper	1/8 tsp.	0.5 mL
Hot water	1 1/2 cups	350 mL
Large eggs	3	3
Grated medium or sharp Cheddar cheese	1 cup	250 mL
Grated Parmesan cheese	1/4 cup	60 mL

TOPPING

Butter or hard margarine	2 tbsp.	30 mL
Dry bread crumbs	1/2 cup	125 mL

MUSHROOM SAUCE

Condensed cream of mushroom soup	10 oz.	284 mL
Canned sliced mushrooms, drained	10 oz.	284 mL
Milk	1/3 cup	75 mL

(continued on next page)

Filling: Melt butter in frying pan. Add onion, oregano and thyme. Sauté until soft.

Stir in next 7 ingredients. Turn into bowl. Set aside.

Pasta: Cook spaghetti in boiling water, cooking oil and salt in large uncovered pot for 10 to 12 minutes until tender but firm. Drain. Return to pot. Set aside.

Sauce: Melt butter in large saucepan. Add onion. Sauté until soft.

Mix in flour, bouillon powder, salt and pepper. Stir in water until it boils and thickens. Remove from heat.

Beat eggs in small bowl until frothy. Stir in both cheeses. Stir into sauce mixture. Add to spaghetti. Pack ½ pasta mixture into greased 8 inch (20 cm) springform pan. Spread filling over top, packing down firmly. Cover with remaining pasta mixture.

Topping: Melt butter in small saucepan. Stir in bread crumbs. Sprinkle over top. Bake in 350°F (175°C) oven for 35 to 40 minutes until browned and heated through. Let stand 10 minutes before removing outside ring of pan.

Mushroom Sauce: Heat and stir all 3 ingredients together. Serve over or with 8 to 10 wedges of cake.

Paré Pointer

A sure way to get bronc-itis is to ride wild horses.

CHICKEN STUFFING PIE

A crustless herb-flavored pie that makes for a good lunch. Add a salad and dinner rolls.

Diced cooked chicken	2 cups	500 mL
Chopped green onion	1/4 cup	50 mL
Finely chopped celery	1/4 cup	50 mL
Small seasoned croutons	1 cup	250 mL
Pepper, sprinkle		
Biscuit mix	3/4 cup	175 mL
Salt	1/2 tsp.	2 mL
Ground thyme	1/4 tsp.	1 mL
Ground sage	1/4 tsp.	1 mL
Milk	1 1/4 cups	275 mL

Spread chicken in bottom of greased 9 inch (22 cm) pie plate. Sprinkle with onion, then celery, croutons and pepper.

Stir biscuit mix, salt, thyme and sage together in bowl. Stir in milk. Pour over all. Bake in 350°F (175°C) oven for 30 to 35 minutes until browned. Serves 4.

MEAL UNDER COVER

This has it all, meat, potatoes and vegetables under a golden crust.

Butter or hard margarine	2 tbsp.	30 mL
Chopped onion	1 1/2 cups	375 mL
All-purpose flour	2 tbsp.	30 mL
Salt	3/4 tsp.	4 mL
Pepper	1/8 tsp.	0.5 mL
Water	1 1/4 cups	275 mL
Worcestershire sauce	2 tsp.	10 mL
Cubed cooked chicken	2 cups	500 mL
Cubed cooked potato	1 cup	250 mL
Sliced cooked carrots	1 cup	250 mL
Cooked peas	1 cup	250 mL
Pastry for covering		

(continued on next page)

Melt butter in frying pan. Add onion. Sauté until soft and browned.

Mix in flour, salt and pepper. Stir in water until it boils and thickens. Add Worcestershire sauce.

Put chicken, potato, carrots and peas into 2 quart (2 L) casserole. Mix lightly. Pour mixture over top.

Roll out pastry a little larger than casserole. Place over top, with pastry about $\frac{1}{2}$ to 1 inch (12 to 24 mm) up sides. Cut several slits in pastry. Bake in 400°F (205°C) oven for about 30 minutes until hot and browned. Serves 4 to 6.

CHICKEN TOURTIÈRE

An excellent variation of this French-Canadian pie.

Ground raw chicken	1½ lbs.	680 g
Finely chopped onion	1 cup	250 mL
Salt	1 tsp.	5 mL
Pepper	¼ tsp.	1 mL
Garlic powder	¼ tsp.	1 mL
Ground sage	¼ tsp.	1 mL
Ground allspice	¼ tsp.	1 mL
Ground cloves	¹⁄₁₆ tsp.	0.5 mL
Water	⅓ cup	75 mL
Medium potatoes	3	3
Boiling water		

Pastry for 2 crust pie

Put first 9 ingredients into saucepan. Cook, stirring occasionally until no pink remains in meat. This will take 10 to 15 minutes.

Peel and quarter potatoes. Cook in some boiling water until tender. Drain. Mash. Add to chicken mixture. Mix. Cool.

Roll ½ pastry and line 9 inch (22 cm) pie plate. Fill with chicken mixture. Roll top crust. Dampen edges and cover with crust. Crimp and trim edges. Cut slits in top. Bake in 400°F (205°C) oven for about 30 minutes until browned. Serves 6.

ROAST CHICKEN

Have an old fashioned Sunday dinner.

Roasting chicken	5 lbs.	2.27 kg
Family Stuffing, page 62	5 cups	1.13 L

Tie wings with string to hold close to body. Pack stuffing lightly into neck and body cavities. Skewer skin together to hold in stuffing. Tie legs to tail. Place in roaster. Cover. Roast in 400°F (205°C) oven for 20 minutes. Reduce heat. Roast in 325°F (160°C) oven for $2\frac{1}{2}$ to 3 hours. Meat thermometer should read 190°F (90°C). Leg joints should move easily. Remove cover last few minutes to brown. If you prefer to cook uncovered, brush skin with softened butter and baste several times during cooking. Make Gravy, page 85. Serves 6 to 8.

CHICKEN ROLLS

Instead of frying, the skin is removed, rolls are crumbed then baked in the oven. Rolled with ham, cheese and tomato.

Large chicken breasts, halved, skin and bones removed	3	3
Thin ham slices	6	6
Cheese slices, halved, mozzarella, Swiss or Cheddar	3	3
Medium tomato, halved, seeded and diced	1	1
Fine dry bread crumbs	$\frac{1}{3}$ cup	75 mL
Grated Parmesan cheese	2 tbsp.	30 mL
Parsley flakes	1 tsp.	5 mL
Ground sage	$\frac{1}{2}$ tsp.	2 mL
Butter or hard margarine, melted	$\frac{1}{4}$ cup	60 mL

(continued on next page)

Pound chicken breast halves between 2 sheets of plastic wrap to make even thickness.

Lay ham slice, ½ cheese slice and ⅙ diced tomato on top. Roll, tucking in sides. Tie with string. Fasten ends with wooden picks.

Stir next 4 ingredients together in small dish.

Brush chicken with butter. Coat with crumb mixture. Place seam side down in 9 x 13 inch (22 x 33 cm) pan. Bake, uncovered, in 350°F (175°C) oven for 45 to 55 minutes until tender. Makes 6 rolls.

TURKEY ROLL

Cooked in jelly roll fashion. Stuffed with carrot and onion.

Carrots, cut in matchsticks	1 lb.	454 g
Chopped onion	1 cup	250 mL
Boiling water		
Parsley flakes	1 tsp.	5 mL
Chicken bouillon powder	1 tsp.	5 mL
Dry bread crumbs	1 cup	250 mL
Finely chopped onion	1 cup	250 mL
Salt	1 tsp.	5 mL
Pepper	¼ tsp.	1 mL
Ground thyme	½ tsp.	2 mL
Water	3 tbsp.	50 mL
Lean ground raw turkey	1½ lbs.	680 g

Cook carrots and onion in some boiling water until tender crisp. Drain. Rinse with cold water. Drain.

Measure next 8 ingredients into bowl. Stir.

Add turkey. Mix. Pat out on waxed paper into 9 x 14 inch (22 x 35 cm) rectangle. Lay carrot sticks parallel to short side of rectangle, spreading them over entire surface. Scatter onion over top. Roll from short end lifting wax paper to help roll. Place seam side down in greased 9 x 13 inch (22 x 33 cm) baking pan. Bake, uncovered, in 350°F (175°C) oven for 1 to 1¼ hours until browned. Brush top with about 1 tsp. (5 mL) cooking oil at half time. Serve with Tomato Sauce, page 55. Serves 8.

Pictured on page 53.

ROAST TURKEY

A turkey is always a good choice, whether or not the occasion is festive.

Turkey	**10 lbs.**	**4.54 kg**
Family Stuffing, page 62		

Pack body and neck cavities loosely with stuffing. Tie wings with string to hold close to body. Skewer skin together to hold in stuffing. Tie legs to tail if they aren't held in place with wire. Place on rack in roaster. Cover with lid or foil.

Roast in 400° (205°C) oven for 30 minutes to get it started. Reduce heat to 325°F (160°C). Allow about 3 hours if unstuffed and about 3¾ hours if stuffed. Meat thermometer inserted in leg, not touching bone, should read 190°F (95°C) when done. Drumstick meat should feel soft and leg should move or twist easily. To brown more, remove cover for last few minutes. If you prefer to cook uncovered, brush skin with softened butter and baste several times during cooking. Serves 12 generously.

TURKEY GRAVY

Drippings with fat from roaster	**¾ cup**	**175 mL**
All-purpose flour	**¾ cup**	**175 mL**
Salt	**¾ tsp.**	**4 mL**
Pepper	**¼ tsp.**	**1 mL**
Drippings without fat plus water	**6 cups**	**1.35 L**
Gravy browner as needed		

Pour all drippings into large measuring cup. Measure first amount and return to large saucepan. Mix in flour, salt and pepper. Pour water mixture into roaster to loosen brown bits. Add to saucepan. Heat and stir until it boils and thickens. Check for salt, adding more if needed. Add a bit of gravy browner if needed.

Every June many girls look on the bride side of life.

A good sauce makes all the difference.

Young domestic duck, quartered	**5 lb.**	**2.27 kg**
PLUM SAUCE		
Strained plums (baby food)	**2 x 4½ oz.**	**2 x 128 mL**
Brown sugar	**2 tbsp.**	**30 mL**
Cider vinegar	**2½ tbsp.**	**40 mL**
Ground cloves	**⅛ tsp.**	**0.5 mL**

Arrange duck portions in roaster. Cover. Roast in 350°F (175°C) oven for about 1½ hours until tender. Drain off fat.

Plum Sauce: Combine next 4 ingredients in bowl. Brush over duck portions. Roast, uncovered, for about 10 minutes to glaze. Brush and roast for another 5 minutes if not glazed enough. Pour rest of sauce over duck on platter. Makes 1 cup (225 mL) sauce. Serves 4.

Adapt this to any meat or poultry.

Fat from drippings	**¼ cup**	**60 mL**
All-purpose flour	**¼ cup**	**60 mL**
Salt	**½ tsp.**	**2 mL**
Pepper	**⅛ tsp.**	**0.5 mL**
Drippings without fat plus water if needed	**2 cups**	**500 mL**
Gravy browner as needed		

To measure fat, pour all drippings into measuring cup or other narrow container. Fat will rise to the top and is easily seen. Spoon off required amount and pour back into pan. Mix in flour, salt and pepper until smooth.

Skim off rest of fat from top of drippings and discard. Stir in drippings and water until it boils and thickens. Add a bit of gravy browner if needed to improve color. Taste for salt and pepper adding more if needed. Makes about 2 cups (500 mL).

40 CLOVE CHICKEN

Turn the fan on the kitchen vent to high, then put this in the oven. Baked garlic imparts a sweet flavor to this delectable chicken. For a go-with, heat some French bread slices and spread with the soft garlic cloves.

Cooking oil	¼ cup	60 mL
Salt	1½ tsp.	7 mL
Pepper	¼ tsp.	1 mL
Parsley flakes	1 tsp.	5 mL
Ground rosemary	½ tsp.	2 mL
Dried tarragon	½ tsp.	2 mL
Ground thyme	½ tsp.	2 mL
Celery flakes	½ tsp.	2 mL
Small onion, quartered	1	1
Roasting chicken, about 4 to 4¼ lbs. (1.81 to 2 kg)	1	1
Garlic cloves, unpeeled	40	40

Measure cooking oil in cup. Stir in next 7 ingredients.

Place onion in chicken cavity. Tie wings to body. Tie legs to tail.

Brush bottom of roaster with cooking oil mixture. Place chicken in center.

Add garlic cloves. Brush chicken and dab garlic with cooking oil mixture. Cover. Roast in 350°F (175°C) oven for about 1½ to 2 hours until tender. Serves 6.

If you want to see snowflakes dance, go watch a snow-ball.

STUFFED CHICKEN BREASTS

It looks like a major effort but it's simple to make.

Butter or hard margarine	2 tbsp.	30 mL
Chopped fresh mushrooms	1 cup	250 mL
Grated carrot	½ cup	125 mL
Finely chopped onion	½ cup	125 mL
Slivered zucchini with peel	1 cup	250 mL
Grated Parmesan cheese	⅓ cup	75 mL
Sherry (or alcohol-free sherry)	2 tbsp.	30 mL
Dijon mustard	1 tbsp.	15 mL
Salt	¾ tsp.	4 mL
Pepper	¼ tsp.	1 mL
Garlic powder	¼ tsp.	1 mL
Parsley flakes	1 tsp.	5 mL
Boneless chicken breast halves	12	12
Large egg	1	1
Water	2 tbsp.	30 mL
Fine dry bread crumbs	1 cup	250 mL
Butter or hard margarine, melted	⅓ cup	75 mL

Melt first amount of butter in frying pan. Add mushrooms, carrot and onion. Sauté until soft.

Add zucchini. Sauté until soft and moisture has cooked away. Remove from heat.

Stir in next 7 ingredients.

Pound chicken flat with meat mallet. Divide filling among 6 pieces. Cover with second pieces of chicken. Pinch edges together.

Beat egg and water with fork in cereal bowl.

Dip chicken in egg mixture and coat with bread crumbs. Drizzle with melted butter. Arrange in greased or greased foil-lined pan large enough to hold in single layer. Bake in 400°F (205°C) oven for about 40 minutes, turning after 20 minutes, until browned and tender. Serves 6 if breasts are small or if large, cut in half to make 12 servings.

SMOKED TURKEY ROAST

It is much more economical to use this variation to smoke your own.

Water	11 cups	2.5 L
Curing salt, not table salt or coarse (pickling) salt	²/₃ cup	150 mL
Coarse (pickling) salt, not table salt	¹/₃ cup	75 mL
Liquid smoke	2¹/₂ tbsp.	37 mL
Onion salt	1 tsp.	5 mL
Garlic salt	¹/₂ tsp.	2 mL
Boneless turkey breast slab	2 lbs.	900 g

Stir first 6 ingredients together in container deeper than height of roast. Stir thoroughly.

Add turkey breast. Put plate over top with clean rock to weigh down. Let marinate in refrigerator for at least 24 hours. Drain. Place in small roaster. Bake, uncovered, in 250°F (120°C) oven for about 2 hours until internal temperature is 180°F (85°C). Makes 6 servings.

SMOKED TURKEY: Double marinade ingredients for 9 pound (4 kg) turkey. Bake breast side down, 1 hour per pound (454 g) in 250°F (120°C) oven until tender. Baste often. Serves 12.

1. Cherry Duckling page 94
2. Bing Cherry Sauce page 94
3. Peach Garnish page 59
4. Stuffed Apples page 57
5. Cranberry Chutney page 63
6. Elegant Chicken page 129
7. Hazelnut Sauce page 129
8. Chicken Wellington page 73
9. Shrimp Stuffing page 60
10. Cornish Hens page 92
11. Wild Rice Stuffing page 66

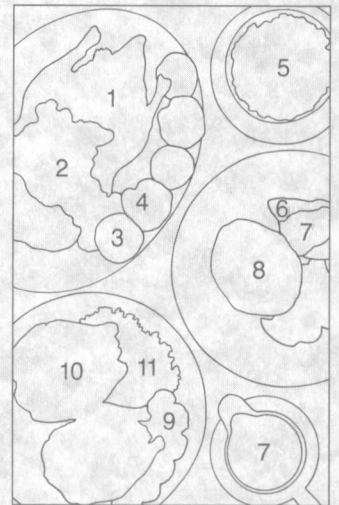

ROAST PHEASANT

Although pheasants aren't too common, they are available from time to time in large grocery stores.

Young pheasants, about 1 lb. (454 g) each	4	4
Potato Stuffing, page 60 or Rice Stuffing, page 59	4 cups	1 L
Bacon slices, halved crosswise (optional)	4	4

If pheasants are larger, allow about 1 pound (454 g) per person in total weight. Fill cavity with stuffing. If you don't stuff each bird, place a few chunks of onion in each cavity. Tie wings and legs close to body. Arrange in roaster. Strips of bacon can be laid over each bird before roasting if desired. Cover. Roast in 325°F (160°C) oven for 1 to 1½ hours. Remove cover near end of cooking to brown. Serves 4.

GRAVY

Pan fat drippings	3 tbsp.	50 mL
All-purpose flour	3 tbsp.	50 mL
Salt	½ tsp.	2 mL
Pepper	⅛ tsp.	0.5 mL
Water	1½ cups	350 mL
Gravy browner		

If pan drippings are scarce, melt 3 tbsp. (50 mL) butter or hard margarine in roaster. Mix in flour, salt and pepper. Add water. Heat and stir until it boils and thickens. Add a bit of gravy browner if needed to make a rich color. Makes 1½ cups (350 mL).

ROAST PIGEON: Prepare and roast the same as for pheasant. Bacon is not necessary.

ROAST QUAIL: Prepare and roast the same as for pheasant. Bacon is optional.

ROAST GROUSE, PARTRIDGE: Prepare and roast the same as for pheasant allowing flexible timing for doneness. A bit of water or chicken bouillon may be added to pan before roasting if birds don't contain much fat.

CORNISH HENS

A meal with flair when you serve an individual bird to each guest.

Cornish hens, about 1 lb. (454 g) each	6	6
Wild Rice Stuffing, page 66 or	6 cups	1.35 L
Family Stuffing, page 62		
Red currant jelly (or orange marmalade)	¼ cup	60 mL

Stuff hens with stuffing of your choice. Skewer skin to keep stuffing in. Tie wings close to body. Tie legs to tail. Put into roaster. Cover. Roast in 350°F (175°C) oven for 30 minutes.

Brush skin with jelly. Continue to roast, uncovered, for about 30 minutes more until tender.

Pictured on page 89.

ROAST TURKEY THIGHS

A different and novel way to serve this economical meat.

Long grain rice	1 cup	250 mL
Chopped onion	½ cup	125 mL
Grated carrot	½ cup	125 mL
Boiling water	2 cups	500 mL
Parsley flakes	1½ tsp.	7 mL
Salt	1 tsp.	5 mL
Ground sage	¼ tsp.	1 mL
Poultry seasoning	¼ tsp.	1 mL
Turkey thighs, boned, flattened slightly	6	6

Cook rice, onion and carrot slowly in boiling water in covered saucepan about 15 minutes until rice is tender and water is absorbed.

Stir in parsley, salt, sage and poultry seasoning.

Divide among thighs using a scant ½ cup (125 mL) each to fill where bones were removed. Tie closed with string. Secure ends with wooden picks. Arrange in small roaster. Cover. Roast in 325°F (160°C) oven for 1½ to 2 hours until tender. Cut each thigh in half to serve 10 to 12.

Variation: Stuff with Family Stuffing, page 62, instead of rice.

About as economical as it gets. Try both sauces. Remove skin if desired.

Turkey wings about 3 lbs. (1.36 kg)	4	4
Barbecue Sauce, page 61, or		
Smokey Sauce, below		

SMOKEY SAUCE

Granulated sugar	1½ tbsp.	25 mL
Salt	1 tsp.	5 mL
Pepper	⅛ tsp.	0.5 mL
Cornstarch	½ tsp.	2 mL
Onion powder	¼ tsp.	1 mL
Ketchup	3 tbsp.	50 mL
White vinegar	1 tbsp.	15 mL
Worcestershire sauce	1½ tsp.	7 mL
Liquid smoke	⅛ tsp.	0.5 mL

Remove wing tips and freeze for soup. Cut wings apart at joint. Arrange in small roaster.

Smokey Sauce: Mix first 5 ingredients in small bowl.

Add remaining 4 ingredients. Stir. Brush over wings. Cover. Roast in 350°F (175°C) oven for 30 minutes. Turn wings and brush with sauce. Cover. Roast for about 30 minutes more until tender. Makes 4 servings.

On being introduced to a centipede, does it put its best foot forward?

CHERRY DUCKLING

The sauce, made from canned cherries, is both colorful and flavorful. Adds a lot to duck.

Small onion, quartered	1	1
Young domestic duck, thawed	5 lbs.	2.27 kg
BING CHERRY SAUCE		
Canned bing cherries, drained, pitted, juice reserved	14 oz.	398 mL
Reserved juice		
Lemon juice, fresh or bottled	1 tbsp.	15 mL
Granulated sugar	3 tbsp.	50 mL
Cornstarch	4 tsp.	20 mL
Water	4 tsp.	20 mL
Red currant jelly	⅓ cup	75 mL

Put onion in duck cavity. Tie wings close to body. Tie legs to tail. Prick skin in several places to allow fat to drain. Place in roaster. Cover. Roast in 350°F (175°C) oven for about 1 to 1¼ hours. Temperature should be 180°F (85°C) in thickest part of meat. Remove to platter and keep warm.

Bing Cherry Sauce: Drain cherry juice into saucepan. Set cherries aside.

Combine next 3 ingredients in saucepan. Heat and stir as you bring to a boil.

Mix cornstarch and water in small bowl. Stir into boiling juice until it returns to a boil and thickens.

Add jelly and cherries. Heat through. Leave duck whole or cut into serving slices or pieces and arrange on platter. Spoon sauce over top or serve on the side. Makes 1¾ cups (400 mL). Duck and sauce serves 6.

Pictured on page 89.

He must be in a band. He plays second fiddle so often.

Enjoy this pricey dish at home.

Young domestic duck, thawed	4 lbs.	1.8 kg
SAUCE		
Granulated sugar	4 tbsp.	60 mL
White vinegar	2 tbsp.	30 mL
Orange juice	1 cup	250 mL
Lemon juice, fresh or bottled	2 tbsp.	30 mL
Grated rind from orange	1	1
Brandy flavoring	½ tsp.	2 mL
Cornstarch	1 tbsp.	15 mL
Water	3 tbsp.	50 mL
Orange slices for garnish		

Tie wings with string to body of duck. Tie legs to tail. Prick skin in several places to allow fat to run out. Set duck in roaster. Cover. Roast in 350°F (175°C) oven for about 1½ hours. Remove cover. Continue to roast until tender and browned.

Sauce: In heavy saucepan cook sugar and vinegar until dark brown. Remove from heat.

Add next 4 ingredients. Stir. Heat again, stirring until it begins to boil.

Mix cornstarch and water together in small cup. Stir into boiling mixture until it returns to a boil and thickens. Keep warm. Makes about 1 cup (225 mL).

Cut duck into serving pieces. Arrange on warmed platter. Pour sauce over top. Tuck orange slices around edge. Serves 4.

A hungry pig eats like a horse. A hungry horse eats like a pig.

ROAST TURKEY DRUMS

Good choice for economy and flavor. Makes a splendid meal.

Turkey drumsticks (about 4)	3¼ lbs.	1.48 kg
Sliced onion	1½ cups	375 mL
Short sticks of celery (4 inch, 10 cm)	8	8
Medium carrots, quartered	4	4
Hot water	1½ cups	375 mL
Chicken bouillon powder	1 tbsp.	15 mL
Tomato sauce	2 x 7½ oz.	2 x 213 mL
Ground thyme	½ tsp.	2 mL
Granulated sugar	½ tsp.	2 mL
Salt	½ tsp	2 mL
Pepper	⅛ tsp.	0.5 mL

Put drumsticks into small roaster. Scatter onion, celery and carrots over top.

Stir hot water and bouillon powder together in bowl. Mix in next 5 ingredients. Pour over top. Cover. Bake in 350°F (175°C) oven for about 2 hours until turkey is tender. Remove turkey to platter. Turn gravy and vegetables into bowl. Serves 4.

CREAMY CHICKEN MOLD

This can hold its place among salads. It can easily double as an appetizer served with toast cups or crackers.

Envelopes unflavored gelatin	3 x ¼ oz.	3 x 7 g
Cold water	¾ cup	175 mL
Condensed chicken broth	10 oz.	284 mL
Salt	¼ tsp.	1 mL
Diced cooked chicken	2 cups	500 mL
Diced celery	½ cup	125 mL
Grated carrot	¼ cup	60 mL
Diced pimiento	2 tbsp.	30 mL
Parsley flakes	1 tsp.	5 mL
Lemon juice, fresh or bottled	2 tbsp.	30 mL
Salad dressing (or mayonnaise)	½ cup	125 mL
Whipping cream (or 1 envelope topping)	1 cup	250 mL

(continued on next page)

Sprinkle gelatin over water in small saucepan. Let stand 1 minute. Heat and stir to dissolve.

Stir in chicken broth and salt. Chill, stirring often, until it begins to thicken.

Fold in next 7 ingredients.

Beat whipping cream until stiff. Fold into gelatin mixture. Turn into 6 cup (1.35 L) mold. Chill.

Pictured on page 143.

CHICKEN GREENS SALAD

Dressed with a piquant oil and vinegar dressing.

Chicken breasts, halved, skin and bones removed	4	4
Cooking oil	1 tbsp.	15 mL
Romaine lettuce, torn or cut bite size	6 cups	1.35 L
Medium tomatoes, diced	3	3
Green onions, chopped	4	4
Medium zucchini, slivered	2	2
HOUSE DRESSING		
Cooking oil	¼ cup	60 mL
White vinegar	2 tbsp.	30 mL
Granulated sugar	½ tsp.	2 mL
Salt	¼ tsp.	1 mL
Prepared mustard	½ tsp.	2 mL
Garlic powder	⅛ tsp.	0.5 mL
Pepper, light sprinkle		
Grated Parmesan cheese	1 tbsp.	15 mL

Brown chicken on both sides in cooking oil in frying pan. Continue to cook until no pink remains.

Toss next 4 ingredients together in large bowl.

House Dressing: Stir all ingredients together well in small bowl. Pour over salad. Toss to coat. Divide among 8 salad plates. Top with warm chicken. It looks better to cut chicken into ½ inch (12 mm) slices before placing over salad. Serves 8.

CHICKEN WALDORF

This variation is an excellent salad. Crunchy, fruity and nutty.

Salad dressing (or mayonnaise)	½ cup	125 mL
Milk	2 tbsp.	30 mL
Granulated sugar	1 tsp.	5 mL
Diced apple, with peel	2 cups	500 mL
Diced cooked chicken	2 cups	500 mL
Diced celery	1 cup	250 mL
Chopped pecans or walnuts	½ cup	125 mL
Raisins	½ cup	125 mL
Salt	¼ tsp.	1 mL
Shredded lettuce (or leaves)	2 cups	500 mL

Mix first 3 ingredients in bowl. Add apple immediately to keep it from turning brown.

Add next 5 ingredients. Stir.

Spread lettuce over large plate or individual plates. Spoon salad over top. Makes 4⅔ cups (1 L).

CHICKEN SALAD

Add dinner rolls for a great lunch.

Diced cooked chicken	3 cups	675 mL
Diced celery	½ cup	125 mL
Chopped green pepper	½ cup	125 mL
Chopped red pepper	½ cup	125 mL
Grated carrot	½ cup	125 mL
Sliced green onion	½ cup	125 mL
Salad dressing (or mayonnaise)	¾ cup	175 mL
Lemon juice, fresh or bottled	2 tsp.	10 mL

Lettuce, cups or shredded
Pimiento strips

Combine first 6 ingredients in bowl. Toss to mix.

In small bowl mix salad dressing and lemon juice. Pour over top. Stir to coat well.

Place lettuce on plate. Add portion of salad. Top with pimiento strips. Makes 6 to 8 servings.

Pictured on page 143.

Delicious served with buttered biscuits or rolls. Makes a good get-together lunch any time of the day or evening.

FIRST LAYER

Envelopes unflavored gelatin	$1\frac{1}{2} \times \frac{1}{4}$ oz.	$1\frac{1}{2} \times 7$ g
Cold water	$\frac{1}{3}$ cup	75 mL
Whole cranberry sauce	14 oz.	398 mL
Crushed pineapple with juice	1 cup	250 mL
Chopped walnuts or pecans	$\frac{1}{2}$ cup	125 mL
Lemon juice, fresh or bottled	1 tbsp.	15 mL

SECOND LAYER

Envelopes unflavored gelatin	$1\frac{1}{2} \times \frac{1}{4}$ oz.	$1\frac{1}{2} \times 7$ g
Cold water	$\frac{1}{3}$ cup	75 mL
Salad dressing (or mayonnaise)	1 cup	250 mL
Water	$\frac{3}{4}$ cup	175 mL
Lemon juice, fresh or bottled	3 tbsp.	50 mL
Salt	$\frac{1}{2}$ tsp.	2 mL
Onion powder	$\frac{1}{4}$ tsp.	1 mL
Diced cooked chicken	2 cups	500 mL
Diced celery	$\frac{1}{2}$ cup	125 mL
Shredded lettuce (or leaves)	2 cups	500 mL

First Layer: Sprinkle gelatin over water in small saucepan. Let stand 1 minute. Heat and stir to dissolve. Pour into bowl.

Add cranberry, pineapple, walnuts and lemon juice. Chill until it begins to thicken. Turn into 8 x 8 inch (20 x 20 cm) pan. Chill until firm.

Second Layer: Sprinkle gelatin over water in small saucepan. Let stand 1 minute. Heat and stir to dissolve.

Add next 7 ingredients in order given. Mix well. Chill until it starts to thicken. Pour over first layer. Chill until firm.

To serve, put shredded lettuce on each plate. Place a square of salad on lettuce. Cuts into 9 pieces.

Paré Pointer

If you really want news to get around, just whisper it to someone.

HOT CHICKEN SALAD

Extra good. Serve at your next luncheon.

Salad dressing (or mayonnaise)	½ cup	125 mL
Milk	2 tbsp.	30 mL
Lemon juice, fresh or bottled	2 tsp.	10 mL
Salt	½ tsp.	2 mL
Onion powder	¼ tsp.	1 mL
Chopped cooked chicken	2 cups	500 mL
Chopped or sliced celery	2 cups	500 mL
Sliced or slivered almonds, toasted in 350°F (175°C) oven about 5 minutes	½ cup	125 mL
Grated medium Cheddar cheese	½ cup	125 mL
Crushed potato chips	½ cup	125 mL

Measure first 5 ingredients into large bowl. Mix.

Add chicken, celery and almonds. Toss well. Divide among 6 small casseroles or put into 1½ quart (1.5 L) casserole.

Sprinkle with cheese. Sprinkle potato chips either around outside edge or evenly over whole surface. Bake, uncovered, in 350°F (175°C) oven for 30 to 40 minutes until heated through. Serves 6.

Pictured on page 143.

CHICKEN AVOCADO SALAD

Extra fruity with raisins and banana. A good addition to a salad luncheon.

Salad dressing (or mayonnaise)	½ cup	125 mL
Granulated sugar	1 tsp.	5 mL
Milk	2 tbsp.	30 mL
Diced cooked chicken	2 cups	500 mL
Diced celery	½ cup	125 mL
Chopped pecans or walnuts	¼ cup	60 mL
Raisins	⅓ cup	75 mL
Salt	¼ tsp.	1 mL
Pepper	⅛ tsp.	0.5 mL
Banana, sliced	1	1
Avocado, sliced	1	1
Bite size lettuce	2 cups	500 mL

(continued on next page)

In medium bowl mix first 3 ingredients.

Add chicken, celery, pecans, raisins, salt and pepper. Stir together well.

Fold in banana and avocado.

Line serving bowl or platter with lettuce. Pile salad on top. Individual plates may be lined with lettuce with salad divided among them. Makes 3⅓ cups (775 mL).

ISLAND SALAD

Make this ahead so it has a few hours to marinate. Good with or without coconut. Try both.

DRESSING
Salad dressing (or mayonnaise)	1 cup	250 mL
Celery flakes	½ tsp.	2 mL
Onion powder	¼ tsp.	1 mL
Milk	2 tbsp.	30 mL
Salt	½ tsp.	2 mL
Pepper	⅛ tsp.	0.5 mL
White vinegar	2 tsp.	10 mL
Curry powder	½ tsp.	2 mL

SALAD
Green onions, chopped	2	2
Diced celery	½ cup	125 mL
Pineapple tidbits, drained	14 oz.	398 mL
Diced cooked chicken	2 cups	500 mL
Cold cooked rice	1 cup	250 mL
Lettuce leaves (or shredded lettuce)	6-8	6-8

Dressing: Mix all 8 ingredients in bowl.

Salad: Combine onions, celery, pineapple, chicken and rice in large bowl. Add dressing. Stir well. Chill for several hours.

Line bowl or plates with lettuce. Pile salad over top. Makes 4 cups (1 L).

Variation: Add ½ cup (125 mL) medium coconut to dressing. It is creamier if you make 1½ times amount of dressing.

Pictured on page 143.

POLYNESIAN CHICKEN SALAD

A wonderful meaty sauce spooned hot over lettuce. Different and so good.

Cooking oil	2 tbsp.	30 mL
Chicken breast, halved, skin and bones removed, cut bite size	1	1
Chicken thighs, skin and bones removed, cut bite size	4	4
Thinly sliced celery	1 cup	250 mL
Green onions, sliced	6	6
Canned bamboo shoots, drained	10 oz.	284 mL
Canned sliced mushrooms, drained	10 oz.	284 mL
Medium tomatoes, cubed	2	2
Soy sauce	3 tbsp.	50 mL
Ground ginger	1/8 tsp.	0.5 mL
Garlic powder	1/8 tsp.	0.5 mL
Salt	1/4 tsp.	1 mL
Cut or torn head lettuce	6 cups	1.35 L

Heat cooking oil in wok or frying pan. Add chicken and celery. Sauté until no pink remains in meat.

Add next 8 ingredients. Stir-fry about 2 minutes.

Divide lettuce among 6 plates. Spoon hot mixture over top. Makes 6 servings.

Pictured on cover.

CHICKEN RICE SALAD

Creamy moist. Contains pineapple. Crunchy good.

Diced cooked chicken	2 cups	500 mL
Crushed pineapple, drained	14 oz.	398 mL
Cold cooked rice	2 cups	500 mL
Diced celery	1/2 cup	125 mL
Salt	1/2 tsp.	2 mL
Pepper	1/8 tsp.	0.5 mL
Salad dressing (or mayonnaise)	1/2 cup	125 mL
Chili sauce	1 tbsp.	15 mL
Lettuce leaves (or shredded lettuce)	4-6	4-6

(continued on next page)

Combine first 6 ingredients in bowl. Stir well.

Mix salad dressing and chili sauce in bowl. Stir. Add to salad. Stir to coat.

Line bowl with lettuce. Pile salad on top. Makes 4 cups (950 mL).

TACO SALAD

It's all here — protein, greens, crispness and good taste.

Lean ground raw chicken	**1 lb.**	**454 g**
Cooking oil	**1 tbsp.**	**15 mL**
Canned kidney beans, with liquid	**14 oz.**	**398 mL**
Envelope taco seasoning mix	**1¼ oz.**	**35 g**
Medium head of lettuce, cut up	**1**	**1**
Medium tomatoes, diced	**1**	**1**
Green onions, sliced	**3**	**3**
Peeled sliced cucumber	**1 cup**	**250 mL**
Ripe avocado, peeled, pitted and **cut in cubes**	**1**	**1**
Pimiento stuffed olives, halved	**12**	**12**
Grated medium Cheddar cheese	**½ cup**	**125 mL**
Bag of plain tortilla chips, crumbled	**6 oz.**	**170 g**
Thousand Island dressing	**1 cup**	**250 mL**

Scramble-fry chicken in cooking oil in frying pan until browned.

Stir in kidney beans and taco seasoning. Cool.

Toss next 7 ingredients in large bowl.

Just before serving add chicken mixture and toss with salad. Mix in tortilla chips and dressing. Serves 10.

There aren't any psychiatrists for dogs because dogs aren't allowed on couches.

CLUBHOUSE SANDWICH

A different twist on an old favorite.

Salad dressing (or mayonnaise)	1 tbsp.	15 mL
Prepared mustard	¼ tsp.	1 mL
Whole wheat bread slices, toasted and buttered	3	3
Cooked chicken slices	2	2
Salt and pepper, sprinkle		
Bacon slices, crispy-fried	2-3	2-3
Lettuce leaf	1	1
Tomato slices	2-3	2-3
Salt and pepper, sprinkle		
Very thin purple onion slice or other sweet mild onion	1	1
Thin slice Swiss or Monterey Jack cheese	1	1
Thin slice medium or sharp Cheddar cheese	1	1
Thin slices of pickle	4	4

Stir salad dressing and mustard together.

On first slice of toast layer chicken, salt and pepper, bacon and lettuce on buttered side. Spread unbuttered side of second slice of toast with ½ mustard mixture. Place mustard side down over lettuce.

On buttered side of second slice of toast layer tomato, salt and pepper, onion, Monterey Jack cheese and Cheddar cheese. Spread remaining mustard mixture on buttered side of third slice and put on top, mustard side down.

Before cutting, press a wooden pick down through each quarter. Cut into quarters. Press pickle slice over each pick. Serve as is or heat in microwave on high for about 10 to 20 seconds to melt cheese a little. Makes 1 sandwich.

The quietest sport is bowling. You can hear a pin drop.

BBQ CHICKEN BUNS

Serve these on the patio for good outdoor fun. Good indoor food as well.

Butter or hard margarine	1 tbsp.	15 mL
Finely chopped onion	½ cup	125 mL
Finely chopped celery	¼ cup	60 mL
Water	½ cup	125 mL
Beef bouillon powder	1 tsp.	5 mL
Ketchup	½ cup	125 mL
White vinegar	2 tsp.	10 mL
Worcestershire sauce	1 tsp.	5 mL
Chili powder	1 tsp.	5 mL
Salt	½ tsp.	2 mL
Pepper	⅛ tsp.	0.5 mL
Chopped pimiento stuffed olives	⅓ cup	75 mL
Chopped cooked chicken	3 cups	700 mL
Kaiser or hamburger buns, split and buttered	12	12

Melt butter in frying pan. Add onion and celery. Sauté until soft.

Add next 10 ingredients. Stir. Heat through.

Spread a scant ¼ cup (50 mL) on each bun. Buns prepared with cooled filling may be wrapped in foil and chilled. To heat, place in 350°C (175°C) oven for about 15 minutes until filling is hot. Makes 12.

Pictured on page 107.

CHICKEN CURRY FILLING

A good sandwich filling with a mild curry flavor.

Finely chopped cooked chicken	2 cups	500 mL
Salad dressing (or mayonnaise)	¼ cup	60 mL
Sour cream	2 tbsp.	30 mL
Curry powder	¼ tsp.	1 mL
Salt	½ tsp.	2 mL

Stir all ingredients together well in bowl. If you want a softer spread, add a bit of milk and mix. Makes 1½ cups (375 mL).

TURKEY BUNWICH

Eat these immediately or heat them in the oven later. Makes good use of leftover turkey.

Butter or hard margarine	1 tbsp.	15 mL
Water	2 tbsp.	30 mL
Sliced or chopped onion	1 cup	250 mL
Diced cooked turkey	2 cups	500 mL
Finely diced celery	1/2 cup	125 mL
Parsley flakes	1 tsp.	5 mL
Salt	1/4 tsp.	1 mL
Pepper, sprinkle		
Salad dressing (or mayonnaise)	1/2 cup	125 mL
Grated medium Cheddar cheese	1/2 cup	125 mL
Hamburger buns, split and buttered	8	8

Melt butter in frying pan. Add water and onion. Cover. Simmer gently, stirring often, until onion is clear and soft and moisture has evaporated.

Put next 7 ingredients into bowl. Mix. Add onion. Stir gently.

Divide among buns. Wrap each bun in foil. Heat in 350°F (175°C) oven for about 15 minutes until heated through. Makes 8 bunwiches.

Pictured on page 107.

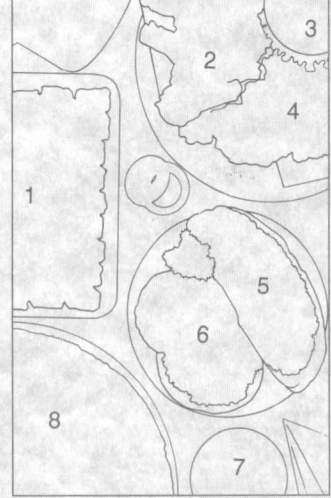

Plates Courtesy Of:
Stokes

Baker Courtesy Of:
The Enchanted Kitchen

Pizza Stone Courtesy Of:
The Enchanted Kitchen

Napkin Rings Courtesy Of:
Dansk Gifts

SANDWICH ROLL

Looks alone will make your mouth water.

White or brown bread slices, toasted and buttered	3	3
Cranberry sauce	1 tbsp.	15 mL
Thin cooked turkey roll slices	3	3
Salt and pepper, sprinkle (optional)		
Tomato slices	2-3	2-3
Salt and pepper, sprinkle (optional)		
Lettuce leaf	1	1
Salad dressing (or mayonnaise)	1-2 tsp.	5-10 mL
Pimiento-stuffed olives and/or pickle slices	2	2

Lay 1 slice toast on cutting board, buttered side up. Spread with cranberry sauce. Shape each turkey slice into roll. Place side by side on cranberry. Sprinkle with salt and pepper. Top with second slice of toast, buttered side down. Butter top side.

Cover with tomato slices, cutting to fit. Sprinkle with salt and pepper. Fold lettuce leaf to fit over tomato. Spread third slice of toast with salad dressing and place face down over lettuce.

Push wooden picks through sides of olives then down through each side of sandwich. Cut in half. Makes 1 sandwich.

Pictured on page 125.

CHICKEN EGG FILLING

A sandwich that contains both the chicken and the egg.

Finely chopped cooked chicken	2 cups	500 mL
Hard-boiled egg, chopped	1	1
Chopped green onion	2 tbsp.	30 mL
Salad dressing (or mayonnaise)	6 tbsp.	100 mL
Salt	$\frac{1}{2}$ tsp.	2 mL
Pepper	$\frac{1}{8}$ tsp.	0.5 mL

Measure all ingredients into bowl. Stir together well. A bit of milk may be added to make a softer spread. Do not freeze. Makes $1\frac{3}{4}$ cups (425 mL).

BREAKFAST BURRITO

A mild burrito dipped in a zesty sauce.

Bacon slice, diced	1	1
Finely chopped onion	1 tsp.	5 mL
Large egg, fork beaten	1	1
Diced cooked chicken (more may be used)	1/4 cup	60 mL
Salt, sprinkle		
Pepper, sprinkle		
Flour tortillas, 7 inch (18 cm)	2	2
Grated medium Cheddar cheese	2 tbsp.	30 mL

Fry bacon and onion until soft.

Add egg, chicken, salt and pepper. Scramble-fry until egg is cooked.

Heat tortillas quickly in another frying pan. Lay on plate. Put half of cheese down center of each. Divide filling between them. Roll. Serve Hot Dipping Sauce, page 57, or Tomato Sauce, page 55, for dipping. Serves 1.

Pictured on page 71.

TURKEY BURGERS

Serve with burger condiments or serve as the meat course for a meal.

Ground raw turkey	1 lb.	454 g
Grated raw potato	1 cup	250 mL
Onion flakes	1 tbsp.	15 mL
Horseradish	2 tsp.	10 mL
Liquid gravy browner	1/4 tsp.	1 mL
Parsley flakes	1/2 tsp.	2 mL
Salt	3/4 tsp.	4 mL
Pepper	1/8 tsp.	0.5 mL
Chicken bouillon powder	1 tsp.	5 mL
Cooking oil	1 tbsp.	15 mL
Hamburger buns, split and buttered	6-8	6-8

Measure first 9 ingredients into bowl. Mix. Shape into 6 to 8 patties.

Fry in cooking oil, browning both sides until no pink remains in meat.

Insert into buns. Makes 6 to 8.

Just filled with good taste.

Salad dressing (or mayonnaise)	1 tbsp.	15 mL
Chili sauce	1 tsp.	5 mL
Sweet pickle relish	¾ tsp.	4 mL
Onion powder, just a pinch		
Pumpernickel or rye bread slices	2	2
Thin slices of cooked chicken, to cover	2-3	2-3
Sauerkraut	3 tbsp.	50 mL
Swiss or mozzarella cheese slice	1	1

Mix first 4 ingredients well in small bowl.

Spread ½ salad dressing mixture over each bread slice. On 1 slice, layer chicken, sauerkraut and cheese. Top with second slice, salad dressing side down. Fry in greased frying pan, browning both sides. Makes 1 sandwich.

SAUCED CLUBHOUSE

An open-faced sandwich with lots of hot cheese sauce ladled over top.

White or whole wheat bread slices, toasted and buttered	6	6
Bacon slices, crispy-fried	12	12
Cooked turkey (or chicken) slices to cover	8-12	8-12
Tomato slices to cover	12-18	12-18
Condensed cheese soup	10 oz.	284 mL
Sour cream	½ cup	125 mL
Sherry (or alcohol-free sherry)	2 tsp.	10 mL
White or whole wheat bread slices, toasted, buttered and halved	6	6

On each of first toast slices on plates layer bacon, turkey and tomato.

Heat and stir soup, sour cream and sherry in saucepan until it reaches a boil. Spoon over top.

Arrange remaining toast slices on edge of plates. Serves 6.

CHICKEN MELT

A colorful open-faced sandwich. A warm tomato slice tops the cheese.

Bread slice, toasted and buttered	1	1
Cooked chicken slices	2-3	2-3
Coleslaw (or drained sauerkraut)	1/3 cup	75 mL
Cheese slice, Cheddar, Swiss or mozzarella	2	2
Tomato slice, warmed in oven, microwave or frying pan	1	1
Dried basil, a wee pinch		
Gherkin pickle or small dill pickle, halved lengthwise	1	1

Put toast on baking pan. Layer with chicken, coleslaw and cheese. Broil to melt cheese.

Transfer to plate. Lay tomato slice on top. Sprinkle with basil.

Overlap pickle halves on the side. Makes 1 sandwich.

Pictured on page 125.

TRENDY TACOS

A good do-it-yourself meal.

Lean ground raw chicken	1 lb.	454 g
Cooking oil	1 tbsp.	15 mL
Chili powder	1½ tsp.	7 mL
Salt	½ tsp.	2 mL
Pepper	⅛ tsp.	0.5 mL
Dried oregano	¼ tsp.	1 mL
Garlic powder	¼ tsp.	1 mL
Paprika	1 tsp.	5 mL
Taco shells	10	10
Diced tomatoes	2	2
Shredded lettuce	1½ cups	375 mL
Onion slivers (optional)	1/3 cup	75 mL
Grated medium or sharp Cheddar cheese	¾ cup	175 mL
Sliced pitted ripe olives (optional)	10	10
Sour cream	⅔ cup	150 mL

(continued on next page)

Scramble-fry chicken in cooking oil until browned.

Add next 6 ingredients. Mix.

Spoon about 2 tbsp. (30 mL) chicken in each taco shell. Add remaining ingredients in layers dividing among the 10 taco shells. Makes 10.

Pictured on page 71.

CHICKEN PIZZA

With pizazz!

CRUST		
Tea biscuit mix	2¼ cups	550 mL
Milk	½ cup	125 mL
TOPPING		
Cooking oil	2 tbsp.	30 mL
Chicken breasts, halved, skin and bones removed	2	2
Chopped onion	1½ cups	350 mL
Small green pepper, seeded and slivered	1	1
Small red pepper, seeded and slivered	1	1
Spaghetti sauce	1⅓ cups	300 mL
Parsley flakes	2 tsp.	10 mL
Dried oregano	1 tsp.	5 mL
Salt	½ tsp.	2 mL
Sliced ripe olives	¼ cup	60 mL
Sliced pimiento stuffed olives	¼ cup	60 mL
Grated mozzarella cheese	2 cups	500 mL

Crust: Stir biscuit mix and milk together to make a soft dough. Pat onto greased 12 inch (30 cm) pizza pan.

Topping: Heat cooking oil in frying pan. Coarsely chop chicken and add along with onion and peppers. Sauté until no pink remains in meat.

Stir spaghetti sauce, parsley, oregano and salt together in small bowl. Spread over crust. Spoon chicken mixture evenly over sauce.

Sprinkle with ripe and stuffed olives. Scatter cheese over all. Bake in 425°F (220°C) oven for about 20 minutes until crust is golden brown. Makes 1 pizza.

Pictured on page 107.

SPICED CHICKEN BUNS

A special lunch to be sure.

Canned sliced peaches with juice	14 oz.	398 mL
Brown sugar, packed	⅓ cup	75 mL
Lemon juice, fresh or bottled	½ tsp.	2 mL
Brandy flavoring	½ tsp.	2 mL
Ground cinnamon	⅛ tsp.	0.5 mL
Butter or hard margarine	¼ cup	60 mL
All-purpose flour	¼ cup	60 mL
Chicken bouillon powder	1 tsp.	5 mL
Salt	½ tsp.	2 mL
Paprika	¼ tsp.	1 mL
Milk	2 cups	500 mL
Sherry (or alcohol-free sherry)	2 tbsp.	30 mL
Coarsely chopped cooked chicken	2 cups	500 mL
Ham slices, cut bun size at least ⅛ inch (3 mm) thick from cooked ham	12	12
Hamburger buns or English muffins, split, toasted and buttered	6	6

Put first 5 ingredients in small saucepan. Stir. Bring to a boil. Simmer 5 minutes. Keep warm.

Melt butter in medium saucepan. Mix in flour, bouillon powder, salt and paprika. Stir in milk until it boils and thickens.

Add sherry and chicken. Return to a simmer.

Lay ham slices over top, overlapping. Cover. Simmer gently to warm ham.

Lay 2 bun halves on each of 6 plates. Using tongs, remove and place ham slice on each half. Spoon about ¼ cup (60 mL) chicken sauce over each. Remove peach slices with slotted spoon and put on top of each bun half. Makes 6 servings of 2 bun halves each.

Prisoners hope they get measles so they will break out.

CRUNCHY CHICKEN FILLING

Celery is added for crunch. Great to have on hand.

Ground cooked chicken	1 cup	250 mL
Finely chopped celery	3 tbsp.	50 mL
Onion powder	1/4 tsp.	1 mL
Parsley flakes	1/2 tsp.	2 mL
Salt	1/4 tsp.	1 mL
Salad dressing (or mayonnaise)	3 tbsp.	50 mL
Milk	3 tbsp.	50 mL

Combine all ingredients in bowl. Stir together well. Store in refrigerator for up to 5 days or freezer for up to 3 months. It is better to freeze without celery. Add after thawing instead. Makes 1 cup (250 mL).

CHICKEN FILLING

Try some variety. Flavorful and crunchy.

Chicken breast, halved	1	1
Water to cover		
Very finely chopped celery	3 tbsp.	50 mL
Lemon juice, fresh or bottled	1/2 tsp.	2 mL
Curry powder, just a pinch		
Salad dressing (or mayonnaise)	2/3 cup	150 mL
Salt	1/8 tsp.	0.5 mL
Toasted almonds, finely chopped (see Note)	3 tbsp.	50 mL

Cover chicken breast halves with water. Bring to a boil, covered. Cook slowly until tender. Drain. When cool enough to handle, remove meat. Discard bone and skin. Chop finely. This gives a better texture than grinding.

Combine remaining ingredients and add to chicken. Stir well. Makes 1 2/3 cups (375 mL).

Note: To toast almonds, spread in pie plate and bake in 350°F (175°C) oven for about 5 minutes. Stir once or twice for even browning.

STROGANOFF BUNS

A scrumptious layer of stroganoff chicken layered with lettuce, tomato and cheese. Good for lunch.

Cooking oil	2 tbsp.	30 mL
Finely chopped onion	1 cup	250 mL
Lean ground raw chicken	1¼ lbs.	570 g
All-purpose flour	⅓ cup	75 mL
Beef bouillon powder	2 tsp.	10 mL
Salt	¾ tsp.	4 mL
Pepper	¼ tsp.	1 mL
Water	1¼ cups	300 mL
Canned sliced mushrooms, drained	10 oz.	284 mL
Worcestershire sauce	¼ tsp.	1 mL
Sour cream	½ cup	125 mL
Hamburger buns, halved, toasted and buttered	7	7
Shredded lettuce	1 cup	250 mL
Thin tomato slices	14	14
Grated medium or sharp Cheddar cheese	⅔ cup	150 mL

Heat cooking oil in frying pan. Add onion and ground chicken. Sauté until no pink remains in meat and onion is soft.

Mix in flour, bouillon powder, salt and pepper. Stir in water until it boils and thickens.

Add mushrooms, Worcestershire sauce and sour cream. Heat through without boiling.

Arrange 2 bun halves on each plate. Top with chicken stroganoff, lettuce, tomato slice and cheese. You may place all items in separate dishes to allow guests to help themselves. Makes 3⅔ cups (825 mL) stroganoff, enough for about 14 bun halves using ¼ cup (60 mL) per half bun.

Don't dream of being something. Stay awake and be.

FRUITY MONTE CRISTO

An unusual sandwich that could even be served for breakfast.

Canned chicken flakes	6.5 oz.	184 g
Coarsely chopped raisins	2 tbsp.	30 mL
Crushed pineapple, drained	¼ cup	60 mL
Salad dressing (or mayonnaise)	1 tbsp.	15 mL
White bread slices, buttered	8	8
Large eggs, beaten	2	2
Water	¼ cup	60 mL
Icing (confectioner's) sugar, sprinkle		

Stir first 4 ingredients together well in bowl.

Divide among 4 bread slices. Cover with remaining 4 slices.

Stir beaten eggs with water in shallow bowl. Dip sandwiches, coating both sides. Brown both sides in well greased frying pan, about 3 minutes per side. Cut each sandwich in half and put on plates.

Sift a bit of icing sugar over top. Makes 4 sandwiches.

Pictured on page 125.

CHICKEN SOUP

Good flavor with vegetables and a hint of pepper.

Chicken stock (see Note)	8 cups	1.8 L
Canned stewed tomatoes, broken up	14 oz.	398 mL
Chopped onion	1 cup	250 mL
Medium carrots, diced or thinly sliced	2	2
Grated raw potato, packed	1 cup	250 mL
Salt	½ tsp.	2 mL
Pepper	½ tsp.	2 mL
Diced cooked chicken	2 cups	500 mL

Put first 7 ingredients into large pot. Bring to a boil, stirring occasionally. Cover. Simmer gently for about 1 hour.

Add chicken. Simmer 5 minutes more. Makes 6⅔ cups (1.5 L).

Note: Chicken stock can be made using 8 cups (1.8 L) water plus 3 tbsp. (45 mL) chicken bouillon powder.

MULLIGATAWNY SOUP

Although carrot and celery aren't in the authentic recipe, they make a colorful addition to Mul-i-gah-TAH-nee soup.

Butter or hard margarine	2 tbsp.	30 mL
Sliced onion	1 cup	250 mL
All-purpose flour	1/3 cup	75 mL
Curry powder	2 tsp.	10 mL
Chicken stock (see Note)	6 cups	1.35 L
Cooking apple, (McIntosh is good) peeled and diced	1	1
Ground cloves, just a pinch		
Diced cooked chicken	2 cups	500 mL
Cream	1/3 cup	75 mL
Leftover cooked rice	3/4 cup	175 mL

Melt butter in large pot. Add onion. Sauté until soft.

Mix in flour and curry powder. Stir in chicken stock until it boils and thickens.

Add apple and cloves. Cover. Simmer for 30 minutes.

Add chicken and cream. Simmer 5 minutes.

Put 2 tbsp. (30 mL) rice in each soup dish. Pour soup over top and serve. Makes 6 3/4 cups (1.5 L) of soup not including rice.

Note: Chicken stock can be made using 6 cups (1.35 L) water plus 2 tbsp. (30 mL) chicken bouillon powder.

QUICK CHICKEN SOUP

Directly from the shelf and freezer.

Condensed chicken broth	2 × 10 oz.	2 × 284 mL
Water	2 1/2 cups	575 mL
Tiny shell pasta, uncooked	1/2 cup	125 mL
Canned chicken, flakes or chunked, broken up	6.5 oz.	184 g
Frozen chopped broccoli	10 oz.	284 g
Grated carrot	1/3 cup	75 mL
Paprika	1/4 tsp.	1 mL

Combine all ingredients in large saucepan. Bring to a boil and simmer, stirring occasionally, about 15 minutes until pasta is tender. Makes 5 1/4 cups (1.2 L).

ORIENTAL CHICKEN SOUP

Clear broth with fine egg threads and vegetables.

Condensed chicken broth	2 x 10 oz.	2 x 284 mL
Water	2½ cups	575 mL
Sliced fresh mushrooms	½ cup	125 mL
Thinly sliced bok choy	1 cup	250 mL
Finely chopped celery	⅓ cup	75 mL
Diced cooked chicken	½ cup	125 mL
Chopped water chestnuts	2 tbsp.	30 mL
Salt	½ tsp.	2 mL
Pepper	⅛ tsp.	0.5 mL
Large egg, beaten frothy	1	1

Combine first 9 ingredients in large saucepan. Bring to a boil. Simmer for 15 minutes.

Add beaten egg slowly in a thin stream to boiling liquid as you whisk with a fork. It will cook in fine threads. Makes 5 generous cups (1.2 L).

Variation: To make soup thicker, mix 2 tsp. (10 mL) cornstarch with 1 tbsp. (15 mL) water. Stir into boiling liquid.

COCK-A-LEEKIE SOUP

Sure to bring out the Scotch in anyone. A full bodied soup.

Chicken stock (see Note)	10 cups	2.25 L
Leeks, white part only, chopped	8	8
Long grain rice, uncooked	¼ cup	60 mL
Quartered pitted dried prunes	1½ cups	375 mL
Parsley flakes	½ tsp.	2 mL
Ground thyme	⅛ tsp.	0.5 mL
Salt	½ tsp.	2 mL
Pepper	¼ tsp.	1 mL
Diced cooked chicken	3 cups	700 mL

Combine first 8 ingredients in large pot. Bring to a boil. Cook slowly for about 30 minutes.

Add chicken. Cover. Cook for another 10 minutes. Check for salt and pepper, adding more if needed. Makes about 14 cups (3.2 L).

Note: Chicken stock can be made using 10 cups (2.25 L) water plus 3⅓ tbsp. (50 mL) chicken bouillon powder.

CREAMY CHICKEN SOUP

Creamy good with a taste of cheese.

Peeled, diced potato	2 1/2 cups	625 mL
Chopped onion	1/2 cup	125 mL
Chopped carrot	1/2 cup	125 mL
Chopped celery	1/2 cup	125 mL
Boiling water		
Condensed cream of mushroom soup	10 oz.	284 mL
Milk	2 1/2 cups	625 mL
Diced cooked chicken	1 cup	250 mL
Worcestershire sauce	1/4 tsp.	1 mL
Parsley flakes	1/4 tsp.	1 mL
Salt	1/4 tsp.	1 mL
Pepper	1/8 tsp.	0.5 mL
Ground thyme	1/8 tsp.	0.5 mL
Grated medium or sharp Cheddar cheese	1 cup	250 mL

Cook potato, onion, carrot and celery in some boiling water until tender. Drain. Mash together.

Add next 8 ingredients. Stir. Heat to a simmer.

Stir in cheese until it melts. Serve. Makes 6 2/3 cups (1.6 L).

Pictured on page125.

CHICKEN NOODLE SOUP

This is not just for sick people. Good soup any time.

Chicken stock (see Note)	8 cups	1.8 L
Diced carrot	1/2 cup	125 mL
Diced celery	1/2 cup	125 mL
Chopped onion	1/2 cup	125 mL
Bacon slices, crispy cooked and crumbled	3	3
Linguine, broken in 1 inch (2.5 cm) lengths, then measured	1 cup	250 mL
Diced cooked chicken	1 1/2 cups	350 mL
Salt	1/4 tsp.	1 mL

(continued on next page)

Put chicken stock, carrot, celery, onion and bacon into large pot. Bring to a boil. Cover. Cook until vegetables are tender.

Add linguine, chicken and salt. Boil, uncovered, for about 15 minutes more until linguine is tender. Makes 8 cups (1.8 L).

Note: Chicken stock can be made using 8 cups (1.8 L) water plus 3 tbsp. (50 mL) chicken bouillon powder.

CHICKEN BORSCHT

A full bodied soup. Excellent choice.

Chicken stock (see Note)	8 cups	1.8 L
Medium carrot, slivered	1	1
Medium parsnip, slivered	1	1
Medium beet, peeled and slivered	1	1
Chopped onion	1 cup	250 mL
Grated raw potato, packed	2 cups	500 mL
Tomato sauce	7½ oz.	213 mL
White vinegar	1 tbsp.	15 mL
Parsley flakes	½ tsp.	2 mL
Dill weed	¼ tsp.	1 mL
Salt	½ tsp.	2 mL
Pepper	⅛ tsp.	0.5 mL
Diced cooked chicken	1 cup	250 mL
Diced cooked ham	1 cup	250 mL
Grated cabbage, packed	3 cups	750 mL
Sour cream, per serving	1 tbsp.	15 mL

Put first 12 ingredients into large pot. Cover and cook slowly for about 20 minutes.

Add chicken, ham and cabbage. Cook, covered, for 10 minutes more.

To each serving, add 1 tbsp. (15 mL) sour cream in center. Makes 12 cups (3 L).

Note: Chicken stock can be made using 8 cups (1.8 L) water plus 3 tbsp. (50 mL) chicken bouillon powder.

Pictured on page 125.

CABBAGE AND CHICKEN SOUP

Quite thick. Tasty and filling.

Chicken stock (see Note)	6 cups	1.35 L
Long grain rice, uncooked	1/3 cup	75 mL
Chopped onion	1/2 cup	125 mL
Ketchup	1 tbsp.	15 mL
Grated cabbage, packed	3 cups	750 mL
Diced cooked chicken	1 cup	250 mL
Salt	1/4 tsp.	1 mL
Pepper, sprinkle		
Grated medium or sharp Cheddar cheese	6 tbsp.	100 mL

In large saucepan combine chicken stock, rice, onion and ketchup. Cover. Cook for about 15 minutes until rice is tender.

Add cabbage, chicken, salt and pepper. Return to a boil. Cook for about 5 minutes to cook cabbage.

Sprinkle each of 6 servings with cheese. Makes 6 1/3 cups (1.4 L).

Note: Chicken stock can be made by using 6 cups (1.35 L) water plus 2 tbsp. (30 mL) chicken bouillon powder.

CHICKEN GUMBO

A full-bodied good gumbo flavored soup.

Chicken stock (see Note)	8 cups	1.8 L
Chopped onion	1 cup	250 mL
Canned tomatoes, broken up	14 oz.	398 mL
Sliced okra	1 cup	250 mL
Small green pepper, seeded and chopped	1	1
Finely chopped celery	1/4 cup	60 mL
Long grain rice, uncooked	1/2 cup	125 mL
Granulated sugar	1 tsp.	5 mL
Salt	1 tsp.	5 mL
Pepper	1/4 tsp.	1 mL
Diced cooked chicken	2 cups	500 mL

Put first 10 ingredients into large pot. Cover. Bring to a boil, stirring often. Boil gently about 20 minutes until rice is cooked.

Add chicken. Heat through. Makes a generous 10 cups (2.25 L).

Note: Chicken stock can be made by using 8 cups (1.8 L) water plus 3 tbsp. (50 mL) chicken bouillon powder.

CHICKEN-VEGETABLE FRY

Serve this stir-fry with steamed rice to round off the meal.

Cooking oil	2 tbsp.	30 mL
Water	2 tbsp.	30 mL
Red wine vinegar	2¹/₂ tbsp.	37 mL
Dried oregano	¹/₂ tsp.	2 mL
Salt	¹/₄ tsp.	1 mL
Garlic powder	¹/₈ tsp.	0.5 mL
Small short thin carrot sticks	1 cup	250 mL
Large chicken breast, halved, skinned and boned, cut bite size	1	1
Broccoli florets	1 cup	250 mL
Cauliflower florets	1 cup	250 mL
Sliced green onion	¹/₃ cup	75 mL
Soy sauce	4 tsp.	20 mL
Cornstarch	¹/₄ tsp.	1 mL
Ground ginger	¹/₂ tsp.	2 mL

Combine first 6 ingredients in wok or frying pan.

Add carrot sticks. Stir-fry on medium-high about 4 minutes until tender crisp.

Add chicken. Stir-fry for 3 to 4 minutes until no pink remains.

Add broccoli, cauliflower and onion. Stir. Cover. Cook on lower heat, stirring occasionally, for 5 minutes.

Mix remaining ingredients in small cup. Add, stirring until it bubbles. Serves 2.

Pictured on page 35.

Appropriately the eye hospital was built on a site for sore eyes.

CHICKEN AND CORN SOUP

Popular with early settlers. Different and delicious.

Chicken stock (see Note)	8 cups	1.8 L
Chopped celery	²⁄₃ cup	150 mL
Corn kernels, fresh or frozen	2 cups	500 mL
Linguine, broken in 1 inch (2.5 cm) pieces, then measured	1 cup	250 mL
Diced cooked chicken	2 cups	500 mL
Salt	¼ tsp.	1 mL
Pepper	⅛ tsp.	0.5 mL
Parsley flakes	½ tsp.	2 mL
Turmeric	¼ tsp.	1 mL
Hard-boiled eggs, chopped	2	2
Whipped cream or frozen whipped topping, for garnish		
Green onion rings, for garnish		

Measure first 10 ingredients into large pot. Bring to a boil. Cover. Cook for about 15 minutes until vegetables are tender.

Garnish each serving with a dab of whipped cream and a few rings of green onion. Makes 9⅓ cups (2.1 L).

Note: Chicken stock can be made by using 8 cups (1.8 L) water plus 3 tbsp. (50 mL) chicken bouillon powder.

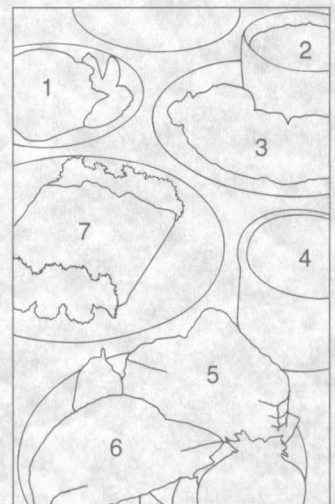

Dishes Courtesy Of:
Le Gnome

WALNUT CHICKEN STIR-FRY

Colorful, nutty, chewy, crispy. Great treat.

Cooking oil	2 tbsp.	30 mL
Chopped onion	1½ cups	350 mL
Thinly sliced celery	1½ cups	350 mL
Small red pepper, seeded and slivered	1	1
Cooking oil	2 tbsp.	30 mL
Chicken breasts, halved, skin and bones removed, slivered	2	2
Chopped walnuts	1 cup	250 mL
Slivered Chinese cabbage	3 cups	750 mL
Sliced water chestnuts, drained	10 oz.	284 mL
Bamboo shoots, drained and sliced	10 oz.	284 mL
Soy sauce	3 tbsp.	50 mL
Sherry (or alcohol-free sherry)	2 tbsp.	30 mL
Granulated sugar	1 tsp.	5 mL
Salt	½ tsp.	2 mL
Garlic powder	¼ tsp.	1 mL
Ground ginger	¼ tsp.	1 mL
Cornstarch	4 tsp.	20 mL
Water	¼ cup	60 mL

Heat first amount of cooking oil in wok or frying pan. Add onion, celery and red pepper. Stir-fry until soft. Turn into bowl.

Add second amount of cooking oil to wok. Add chicken. Stir-fry until no pink remains in meat.

Add walnuts and cabbage. Stir-fry 4 minutes to wilt cabbage.

Add next 8 ingredients along with onion mixture. Stir-fry for 5 minutes.

Mix cornstarch with water in small cup. Add and stir until thickened and glazed. Makes 6½ cups (1.5 L).

Pictured on page 35.

Paré Pointer

It is odd how you can blaze a trail and burn up the road.

CHICKEN STIR-FRY

Serve this colorful dish with noodles or rice for a full meal.

Cooking oil	2 tbsp.	30 mL
Chicken breasts, halved, skin and bones removed, slivered or cubed	2	2
Medium onion, sliced in thin rings	1	1
Thinly sliced carrot coins	1 cup	250 mL
Thinly sliced celery	½ cup	125 mL
Coarsely chopped fresh mushrooms	1 cup	250 mL
Medium zucchini, with peel, slivered or cubed	2	2
Water	2 tbsp.	30 mL
Snow peas, fresh or frozen, thawed	6 oz.	170 g
Green pepper, seeded and slivered	1	1
Fresh grated ginger (or ¼ tsp., 1 mL, powdered)	1 tsp.	5 mL
Green onions, sliced	2-3	2-3
Cornstarch	2 tsp.	10 mL
Soy sauce	2 tsp.	10 mL
Sherry (or alcohol-free sherry)J131	2 tbsp.	30 mL
Salt	½ tsp.	2 mL
Cayenne pepper	⅛ tsp.	0.5 mL

Heat cooking oil in wok or large frying pan. Add chicken. Stir-fry until no pink remains. Turn into bowl.

Add next 6 ingredients to wok. Cover. Steam about 5 minutes until tender crisp.

Add peas, green pepper, ginger and onions. Stir-fry about 5 minutes to soften. Add chicken. Heat through.

Mix cornstarch, soy sauce, sherry, salt and cayenne pepper together. Stir into wok contents to thicken and coat. Makes 6½ cups (1.5 L).

Pictured on page 35.

He decided it was easier to do his task right than to explain all the reasons why he didn't.

Incredibly good. The sauce does it.

All-purpose flour	2 tbsp.	30 mL
Salt	1/8 tsp.	0.5 mL
Pepper, just a pinch		
Paprika	1/8 tsp.	0.5 mL
Hard margarine (butter browns too fast)	1 tbsp.	15 mL
Boneless chicken breast halves	4	4
HAZELNUT SAUCE		
Sliced fresh mushrooms	1 cup	250 mL
White wine (or alcohol-free wine)	1/2 cup	125 mL
Condensed cream of mushroom soup	1/2 x 10 oz.	1/2 x 284 mL
Garlic powder	1/4 tsp.	1 mL
Sliced hazelnuts, toasted	2 tbsp.	30 mL

Combine flour, salt, pepper and paprika in saucer. Mix. Place in paper bag.

Melt margarine in frying pan. Coat chicken with flour mixture shaking 2 or 3 pieces at a time in bag. Cook and brown chicken until no pink remains. Remove to serving bowl. Keep warm.

Hazelnut Sauce: In same frying pan add mushrooms and wine. Stir to loosen brown bits. Boil gently for 3 to 4 minutes to soften mushrooms and reduce liquid.

Stir in soup, garlic powder and hazelnuts. Return to a boil. Pour over chicken. Makes 4 servings.

Pictured on page 89.

All the nuts gather at the Hershey Bar.

BRUNSWICK STEW

Contains a different vegetable combination. Includes lima beans.

Bacon slices, diced	4	4
Chopped onion	2½ cups	575 mL
Chicken parts, skin removed	4 lbs.	1.8 kg
Boiling water, just to cover		
Chicken bouillon powder	2 tbsp.	30 mL
Canned tomatoes, broken up	2 × 14 oz.	3 × 398 mL
Medium potatoes, cubed	3	3
Kernel corn, fresh or frozen	2 cups	500 mL
Canned lima beans, drained	14 oz.	398 mL
Worcestershire sauce	2 tsp.	10 mL
Salt	½ tsp.	2 mL
Pepper	¼ tsp.	1 mL
Cayenne pepper	⅛ tsp.	0.5 mL

Fry bacon and onion in frying pan. Transfer with slotted spoon to large pot.

Add chicken, boiling water and bouillon powder. Bring to a boil. Cover. Simmer for about 45 minutes until chicken is tender. Remove chicken with slotted spoon. When cool enough to handle, remove bones. Cut meat into bite size pieces. Return to pot.

Add next 8 ingredients. Cook, uncovered, until potato is tender and stew has thickened. This will take about 20 minutes. Makes 12 cups (2.7 L).

The only fat-free thing worth eating now and then is your pride.

This is a medium flavored chili. Add more chili to taste if you like.

Cooking oil	2 tbsp.	30 mL
Chopped onion	2 cups	500 mL
Lean ground raw chicken	2 lbs.	1.8 kg
All-purpose flour	2 tbsp.	30 mL
Canned tomatoes, broken up	14 oz.	398 mL
Canned kidney beans	2 × 14 oz.	2 × 398 mL
Chili powder	1 tbsp.	15 mL
Beef bouillon powder	1 tbsp.	15 mL
Salt	1 tsp.	5 mL
Pepper	$\frac{1}{4}$ tsp.	1 mL
Dried oregano	$\frac{1}{4}$ tsp.	1 mL
Granulated sugar	$\frac{1}{2}$ tsp.	2 mL
Worcestershire sauce	$\frac{1}{2}$ tsp.	2 mL

Heat cooking oil in frying pan. Add onion and ground chicken. Scramble-fry until browned.

Mix in flour. Stir in tomatoes until it boils.

Put next 8 ingredients into Dutch oven. Add chicken mixture. Stir. Bring to a boil and simmer for 30 minutes. Stir often as it simmers. Makes $7\frac{2}{3}$ cups (1.73 L).

Ships have always used knots instead of miles to keep the ocean tide.

DRUM BEAT

So colorful and appetizing with a chutney-type sauce.

All-purpose flour	¼ cup	60 mL
Chicken bouillon powder	1 tsp.	5 mL
Cooking oil	2 tbsp.	30 mL
Chicken drumsticks	8	8
Chopped onion	2 cups	500 mL
Reserved flour mixture		
Garlic powder	½ tsp.	2 mL
Canned tomatoes, broken up	14 oz.	398 mL
Water	1 cup	250 mL
White vinegar	⅓ cup	75 mL
Brown sugar, packed	⅓ cup	75 mL
Ketchup	1 tbsp.	15 mL
Coarsely chopped raisins	¼ cup	60 mL
Salt	½ tsp.	2 mL
Pepper	¼ tsp.	1 mL
Ground cinnamon	¼ tsp.	1 mL
Ground ginger	⅛ tsp.	0.5 mL
Frozen peas	2 cups	500 mL
Canned kernel corn, drained	12 oz.	341 mL

Stir flour and bouillon powder together in small bowl.

Heat cooking oil in frying pan. Coat drumsticks with flour mixture, reserving unused mixture. Brown both sides of drumsticks. Remove to plate.

Add onion to frying pan. Sauté until soft, adding more cooking oil if needed.

Mix in reserved flour mixture. Stir in garlic powder, tomatoes and water until it boils and thickens.

Add next 8 ingredients. Stir. Add drumsticks. Cover. Simmer for about 45 minutes until chicken is tender.

Add peas and corn. Stir. Cover. Simmer for 3 to 4 minutes until peas are cooked. Serves 4.

An old classic. Allow extra time to prepare.

Large chicken breasts, halved, skin and bones removed	4	4
Parsley flakes	1 tbsp.	15 mL
Chives	1 tbsp.	15 mL
Worcestershire sauce	1/2 tsp.	2 mL
Salt	1/2 tsp.	2 mL
Pepper	1/4 tsp.	1 mL
Garlic powder (or 1/2 clove, minced)	1/8 tsp.	0.5 mL
Butter or hard margarine, softened	1/2 cup	125 mL
All-purpose flour	1/3 cup	75 mL
Large eggs, beaten	2	2
Fine dry bread crumbs	1 cup	250 mL
Cooking oil for deep-frying		
MUSHROOM SAUCE		
Butter or hard margarine	2 tbsp.	30 mL
Sliced fresh mushrooms	2 cups	500 mL
All-purpose flour	2 tsp.	10 mL
Chicken bouillon powder	1 tsp.	5 mL
Paprika	1/8 tsp.	0.5 mL
Light cream	3/4 cup	175 mL
Soy sauce	1 tsp.	5 mL

Pound each chicken breast between 2 sheets of waxed paper to flatten 1/4 inch (6 mm) thick. Do not puncture or tear.

In small bowl mix next 7 ingredients. Shape into 8 balls or rectangular shapes. Chill in freezer for a few minutes until firm. Place ball at long (wide) end of each breast. Fold sides over first then bring up front and back fastening with wooden picks.

Roll in flour, dip in egg and coat with crumbs. Chill for about 1 hour.

Deep-fry, 2 at a time, in 375°F (190°C) hot oil for about 3 minutes until golden. Drain on paper towels.

Mushroom Sauce: Melt butter in frying pan. Add mushrooms. Sauté until soft.

Mix in flour, bouillon powder and paprika. Stir in cream and soy sauce until it boils. Spoon over chicken. Makes 8 servings.

Variation: For a simple filling, mix butter with 2 tbsp. (30 mL) chopped chives.

NUTTY CHICKEN SCALLOPS

This will be the hit of a dinner party. Sauce is exquisite.

All-purpose flour	3 tbsp.	50 mL
Salt	½ tsp.	2 mL
Pepper	⅛ tsp.	0.5 mL
Paprika	½ tsp.	2 mL
Large chicken breasts, halved, skin and bones removed	3	3
Hard margarine (butter browns too fast)	2 tbsp.	30 mL
NUTTY SAUCE		
Butter or hard margarine	2 tbsp.	30 mL
Sliced fresh mushrooms	2 cups	500 mL
All-purpose flour	2 tbsp.	30 mL
Salt	½ tsp.	2 mL
Pepper	¼ tsp.	1 mL
Garlic powder	¼ tsp.	1 mL
Apple juice	¾ cup	175 mL
Milk	1 cup	250 mL
Sliced hazelnuts toasted in 350°F (175°C) oven	3 tbsp.	50 mL

Shake first 4 ingredients together in paper bag.

Add 2 to 3 chicken pieces at a time. Shake in bag to coat.

Heat margarine in frying pan. Add chicken. Brown on both sides until tender, about 8 to 10 minutes. Transfer to heated platter. Keep warm.

Nutty Sauce: Add butter to same frying pan. Add mushrooms. Sauté to brown.

Mix in flour, salt, pepper and garlic powder. Stir in apple juice until it boils and thickens. Simmer until very thick.

Stir in milk and hazelnuts. Simmer about 2 minutes. Spoon over chicken. Serves 6.

Paré Pointer

Those workers aren't paid what they're worth and they are very happy about it.

Try both the dry coating and the egg coating. Egg coating is especially good if the skin is removed.

SIMPLE COATING

All-purpose flour	⅓ **cup**	**75 mL**
Paprika	**1 tsp.**	**5 mL**
Salt	**1 tsp.**	**5 mL**
Pepper	¼ **tsp.**	**1 mL**
Cooking oil	**2 tbsp.**	**30 mL**
Chicken parts	**3 lbs.**	**1.36 kg**

Measure first 4 ingredients into cereal bowl. Stir.

Heat cooking oil in frying pan. Roll damp chicken in flour mixture. Brown both sides well. Lower heat and cover. Cook so it is barely frying for about 20 minutes more until tender. Turn often. Serves 4 to 6.

EGG COATING

Large egg, fork beaten	**1**	**1**
Milk	½ **cup**	**125 mL**
Salt	¾ **tsp.**	**4 mL**
Pepper	¼ **tsp.**	**1 mL**
Fine dry bread crumbs	⅓ **cup**	**75 mL**
Paprika	¾ **tsp.**	**4 mL**

Combine first 4 ingredients in cereal bowl.

Mix crumbs and paprika in second bowl. Dip chicken in egg mixture and coat with crumb mixture. Cook as above.

DEEP FRIED CHICKEN: Use young fryers that have small size parts. Coat in Simple Coating, above. Deep fry in hot 375°F (190°C) fat for about 10 minutes until both sides are cooked and browned.

Paré Pointer

He didn't mind it if his bride made sacrifices for him as long as it wasn't burnt offerings.

SHRIMPY CHICKEN AND RICE

This combination is excellent over rice and equally good over noodles.

RICE

Long grain rice	1½ cups	375 mL
Boiling water	3 cups	750 mL
Salt	½ tsp.	2 mL

SHRIMP SAUCE

Butter or hard margarine	4 tbsp.	60 mL
Sliced fresh mushrooms	2 cups	500 mL
Finely chopped onion	3 tbsp.	50 mL
All-purpose flour	¼ cup	60 mL
Evaporated skim milk (or half and half)	13½ oz.	385 mL
Milk	⅔ cup	150 mL
Cooked shrimp (or 4 oz., 114 g can)	1 cup	250 mL
Coarsely chopped cooked chicken	2 cups	500 mL
Chopped chives	2 tbsp.	30 mL
Sherry (or alcohol-free sherry)	2 tbsp.	30 mL
Chopped pimiento	2 tbsp.	30 mL

Rice: Cook rice in boiling water and salt about 15 minutes until tender and water is absorbed.

Shrimp Sauce: Melt butter in frying pan. Add mushrooms and onion. Sauté until soft.

Mix in flour. Stir in both milks until it boils and thickens.

Add shrimp, chicken and chives. Stir. Heat through.

Stir in sherry and pimiento. Makes 4 cups (1 L).

The reason cities are referred to as "she" is because they all have outskirts.

Lots of meat in this loaf. Use for sandwiches as well as for a cold plate. Easy to get a commercial look to the slices.

Dark and white chicken parts	**4 lbs.**	**1.82 kg**
Medium onion, quartered	**1**	**1**
Celery ribs, quartered	**3**	**3**
Medium carrots, quartered	**2**	**2**
Bay leaves	**2**	**2**
Parsley flakes	**1 tsp.**	**5 mL**
Water to cover		
Cold reserved chicken broth	**½ cup**	**125 mL**
Unflavored gelatin powder	**2 x ¼ oz.**	**2 x 7 g**
Cold reserved chicken broth	**3¼ cups**	**725 mL**
Salt	**1 tsp.**	**5 mL**
Pepper	**¼ tsp.**	**1 mL**
Seasoned salt	**1 tsp.**	**5 mL**

Put first 7 ingredients into Dutch oven. Cover. Cook for about 50 minutes until meat is very tender. Remove from pot. Strain chicken broth into tall narrow container. Remove fat. Reserve broth. Discard skin and bones. Dice meat or cut in slivers. You should have 6 cups (1.35 L). Turn into 9 x 5 x 3 inch (23 x 12 x 7 cm) loaf pan.

Measure first amount of broth. Sprinkle gelatin over cold broth in saucepan. Let stand 1 minute.

Add remaining ingredients. Heat and stir to dissolve gelatin. Pour over chicken. Place in refrigerator. As gelatin thickens be sure to push meat gently below surface. Chill several hours or overnight. Serve in slices. Makes 1 loaf.

Pictured on page 125.

He keeps laughing up his sleeve now that he knows where his funny bone is.

FOREIGN STEW

Rice from abroad and pumpkin from down under bring a new flavor sensation to stew.

Chicken parts	3 lbs.	1.36 kg
Water to cover		
Beef bouillon powder	2 tbsp.	30 mL
Salt	1 tsp.	5 mL
Pepper	1/4 tsp.	1 mL
Medium potatoes, cut in 8 pieces each	4	4
Long grain rice, uncooked	1/2 cup	125 mL
Medium onions, sliced	2	2
Pumpkin or yellow squash cubes	1 cup	250 mL
Peas, fresh or frozen	1 cup	250 mL
Garlic powder	1/4 tsp.	1 mL

Place first 5 ingredients in large pot. Cover. Bring to a boil. Simmer for 30 minutes.

Add remaining ingredients. If it looks as though there is too much liquid, reserve a cupful and add later if needed. Cover. Return to a boil. Boil slowly for about 30 minutes until vegetables are tender. Makes 14 cups (3.15 L).

CHICKEN SCHNITZELS

Looks great. Tender and easy. Increases readily.

Boneless chicken breast halves, skin removed	8	8
All-purpose flour, generous measure	1/3 cup	75 mL
Paprika	1 tsp.	5 mL
Salt	1 tsp.	5 mL
Pepper	1/4 tsp.	1 mL
Large eggs, fork beaten	2	2
Water	2 tbsp.	30 mL
Fine dry bread crumbs	3/4 cup	175 mL
Cooking oil	2 tbsp.	30 mL

(continued on next page)

Place chicken between 2 pieces plastic wrap. Pound as thin as you can without separating.

Mix flour, paprika, salt and pepper in shallow dish.

Stir eggs and water together in small bowl.

Place bread crumbs on plate.

Heat cooking oil in frying pan. Dip chicken in flour mixture, then in egg mixture, then in bread crumbs. Fry, browning both sides well until meat is tender. Makes 8 servings.

CHICKEN À LA KING

Wonderful chafing dish special. Serve over biscuits or in puff pastry shells. Colorful red and green bits show through.

Butter or hard margarine	6 tbsp.	100 mL
Sliced fresh mushrooms	1 cup	250 mL
Chopped green pepper	1	1
All-purpose flour	6 tbsp.	100 mL
Chicken bouillon powder	2 tsp.	10 mL
Salt	¾ tsp.	4 mL
Pepper	⅛ tsp.	0.5 mL
Milk	1½ cups	375 mL
Water	1½ cups	375 mL
Diced cooked chicken	3 cups	750 mL
Chopped pimiento	¼ cup	60 mL
Sherry (or alcohol-free sherry)	¼ cup	60 mL

Melt butter in frying pan. Add mushrooms and green pepper. Sauté until soft.

Mix in flour, bouillon powder, salt and pepper. Using twice as much pepper zips it up. Stir in milk and water until it boils and thickens.

Add chicken, pimiento and sherry. Stir. Heat through. Makes 5½ cups (1.25 L).

Pictured on page 125.

TURKEY À LA KING: Add 1 cup (250 mL) cooked peas. Use turkey instead of chicken.

CHICKEN MOLE

A MOH-lay that cooks on top of the stove. Spice is just right but if you want you can add more pepper sauce.

Chicken breasts, halved, skin and bones removed	3	3
Hard margarine (butter browns too fast)	2 tbsp.	30 mL
Medium onion, chopped	1	1
Green pepper, chopped	1	1
Tomato sauce	2 × 7½ oz.	2 × 213 mL
Ground almonds	¼ cup	60 mL
Chili powder	2 tsp.	10 mL
Salt	1 tsp.	5 mL
Pepper	¼ tsp.	1 mL
Whole cloves	2	2
Hot pepper sauce	¼ tsp.	1 mL
Garlic powder	¼ tsp.	1 mL
Unsweetened baking chocolate half square, cut up	½ × 1 oz.	½ × 28 g

Brown chicken in margarine in frying pan. Cut into bite size pieces.

Add remaining ingredients. Heat and stir until chocolate is melted and mixture is simmering. Cover. Simmer for 30 minutes. Makes 6 servings.

BLACKENED CHICKEN

This might set off your smoke detector. Turn kitchen fan on high. Delicious and so easy. Better to pan-fry on the barbecue.

Salt	1 tbsp.	15 mL
Paprika	1 tbsp.	15 mL
Pepper	1 tsp.	5 mL
Garlic powder	½ tsp.	2 mL
Onion powder	½ tsp.	2 mL
Ground thyme	½ tsp.	2 mL
Chili powder	½ tsp.	2 mL
Dried oregano	½ tsp.	2 mL
Cayenne pepper	½ tsp.	2 mL
Boneless chicken breast halves	6	6
Butter or hard margarine, melted	3 tbsp.	50 mL

(continued on next page)

Mix first 9 ingredients in cereal bowl.

Pound chicken breasts between 2 pieces of waxed paper to ¼ inch (6 mm) thick.

Heat heavy frying pan (not coated) until drops of water bounce all over pan. Brush chicken with butter. Sprinkle liberally with seasoning on both sides. This is easier to do if you have an extra salt shaker on hand. Place 2 or 3 pieces in pan. When blackened, turn other side. Cooks quickly and is cooked as soon as it blackens on both sides. Makes 6 servings.

MIXED CHICKEN STEW

Two kinds of potatoes and lots of vegetables in this.

Chicken parts, skin removed	3 lbs.	1.36 kg
Water to cover		
Chicken bouillon powder	2 tbsp.	30 mL
Ketchup	1 tbsp.	15 mL
Medium onions, cut in chunks	2	2
Medium carrots, sliced	3	3
Sliced celery	½ cup	125 mL
Medium potatoes, cubed	3	3
Sweet potatoes, sliced or cubed	1 lb.	454 g
Coarsely grated cabbage, packed	3 cups	750 mL
Salt	1½ tsp.	7 mL
Pepper	¼ tsp.	1 mL
Garlic powder	¼ tsp.	1 mL
Ground thyme	½ tsp.	2 mL

Put chicken into large pot. Add water to cover. Add bouillon powder. Cover. Bring to a boil. Simmer for about 30 minutes until tender. Remove chicken with slotted spoon. Remove bones. Cut meat bite size and return to pot.

Add remaining ingredients. If it looks like too much liquid, reserve a cupful and add as needed. Cover. Cook slowly for about 1 hour. Makes 12 cups (2.7 L).

CHICKEN STROGANOFF

This is good enough to eat alone but to make it go further, serve it with rice, noodles or mashed potatoes.

Cooking oil	2 tbsp.	30 mL
Sliced fresh mushrooms	2 cups	500 mL
Chicken breasts, halved, skin and bones removed, cut in 2 inch (5 cm) strips	2	2
Chopped onion	1 cup	250 mL
All-purpose flour	2 tbsp.	30 mL
Salt	$\frac{1}{2}$ tsp.	2 mL
Pepper	$\frac{1}{4}$ tsp.	1 mL
Paprika	$\frac{1}{2}$ tsp.	2 mL
Parsley flakes	$\frac{1}{2}$ tsp.	2 mL
Beef bouillon powder	1 tbsp.	15 mL
Water	$1\frac{1}{4}$ cups	300 mL
Sour cream	1 cup	250 mL

Heat cooking oil in frying pan. Add mushrooms, chicken and onion. Sauté until no pink remains in meat and onions are soft.

Mix in next 6 ingredients. Stir in water until it boils and thickens.

Add sour cream. Stir. Heat without boiling. Serve with noodles or rice. Makes $3\frac{2}{3}$ cups (825 mL).

1. Island Salad page 101
2. Creamy Chicken Mold page 96
3. Irish Wheat Bread page 63
4. Hot Chicken Salad page 100
5. Chicken Salad page 98

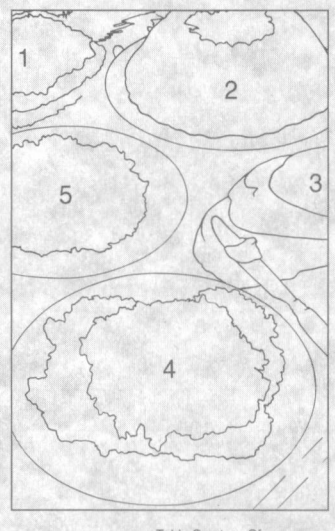

CHICKEN CROQUETTES

Fantastic flavor to these golden bundles.

Large eggs	2	2
Condensed cream of chicken soup	10 oz.	284 mL
Dry bread crumbs	1 cup	250 mL
Onion flakes	2 tbsp.	30 mL
Poultry seasoning	1/4 tsp.	1 mL
Parsley flakes	1/2 tsp.	2 mL
Celery flakes	1/8 tsp.	0.5 mL
Salt	1/4 tsp.	1 mL
Chicken bouillon powder	1 tsp.	5 mL
Ground or finely chopped cooked chicken	1 1/2 cups	375 mL
All-purpose flour	1/4 cup	60 mL
Large egg	1	1
Water	1 tbsp.	15 mL
Fine dry bread crumbs	1/2 cup	125 mL
Cooking oil for deep frying		
MUSHROOM SAUCE		
Condensed cream of mushroom soup	10 oz.	284 mL
Milk	1/2 cup	125 mL
Worcestershire sauce	1/4 tsp.	1 mL
Paprika	1/8 tsp.	0.5 mL

Beat eggs with spoon in bowl. Mix in soup. Add next 8 ingredients. Stir. Chill for 2 hours.

Put flour into another small bowl.

Beat third egg and water with fork in another bowl.

Put bread crumbs into a fourth bowl. Measure 1/4 cup (60 mL) chicken portions. An ice cream scoop works well. Coat chicken portion with flour, dip in egg and coat with crumbs. Shape into mounds.

Deep-fry in hot 375° (190°C) cooking oil until golden brown. Serve hot with Mushroom Sauce. Makes 10.

Mushroom Sauce: Heat and stir all ingredients in saucepan. Serve with croquettes. Makes 1 1/2 cups (350 mL).

CHICKEN SAUSAGE PATTIES

Not just a chicken flavor, but an extra flavored patty kids will love.

Finely chopped onion	¹/₂ cup	125 mL
Brown sugar	2 tbsp.	30 mL
Soy sauce	1 tbsp.	15 mL
Seasoned salt	³/₄ tsp.	4 mL
Garlic powder	¹/₄ tsp.	1 mL
Ground sage	¹/₂ tsp.	2 mL
Dry bread crumbs	¹/₃ cup	75 mL
Ground raw chicken	1 lb.	454 g

Measure first 7 ingredients in medium bowl. Mix well.

Add chicken. Mix thoroughly. Divide into 8 patties. Fry in greased frying pan until no pink remains in meat. Makes 8 patties.

CHICKEN CREOLE

Brown and cook in the same pan. Colorful.

Cooking oil	2 tbsp.	30 mL
Chicken parts	3 lbs.	1.36 kg
Canned tomatoes, broken up	14 oz.	398 mL
Chopped onion	1 cup	250 mL
Chopped celery	¹/₂ cup	125 mL
Green pepper, seeded and thinly sliced	1	1
Sliced fresh mushrooms	2 cups	500 mL
Salt	1 tsp.	5 mL
Pepper	¹/₄ tsp.	1 mL
Ground thyme	¹/₂ tsp.	2 mL

Heat cooking oil in frying pan. Add chicken. Brown both sides well.

Add remaining ingredients. Bring to a boil. Cover. Simmer slowly for 30 to 45 minutes until chicken is tender. Serves 4 to 6.

Pictured on page 53.

A touch of gourmet.

Chicken breasts, halved, skin and bones removed	2	2
All-purpose flour	¼ cup	60 mL
Hard margarine (butter browns too fast)	2 tbsp.	30 mL
Salt, sprinkle		
Pepper, sprinkle		
SHRIMP SAUCE		
Butter or hard margarine	3 tbsp.	50 mL
All-purpose flour	3 tbsp.	50 mL
Salt	½ tsp.	2 mL
Pepper	⅛ tsp.	0.5 mL
Onion powder	⅛ tsp.	0.5 mL
Dill weed	⅛ tsp.	0.5 mL
Milk	1 cup	250 mL
Salad dressing (or mayonnaise)	¼ cup	60 mL
Canned small shrimp, rinsed and drained	4 oz.	113 g

Pound chicken between 2 pieces of waxed paper or plastic to make fairly thin.

Coat with flour and cook in margarine in frying pan, browning both sides. Sprinkle with salt and pepper.

Shrimp Sauce: Melt butter in saucepan. Mix in flour, salt, pepper, onion powder and dill weed.

Stir in milk and salad dressing until it boils and thickens.

Carefully stir in shrimp. Heat through. Serve over chicken. Serves 4.

Always buy a thermometer in the winter. It is a lot lower then.

CHICKEN PATTIES

Quick and easy.

Large egg	1	1
Dry bread crumbs	1 cup	250 mL
Milk	1/2 cup	125 mL
Seasoned salt	1 tsp.	5 mL
Ground raw chicken	1 1/2 lbs.	680 g
All-purpose flour	1/2 cup	125 mL
Large egg	1	1
Water	2 tbsp.	30 mL
Dry fine bread crumbs	1/2 cup	125 mL
Paprika	1 tsp.	5 mL
Hard margarine (butter browns too fast)	2 tbsp.	30 mL

Beat first egg with spoon in medium bowl. Add next 3 ingredients. Stir.

Add chicken. Mix. Shape into 9 patties.

Place flour in small bowl.

Beat second egg with fork in second small bowl. Mix in water to make egg wash.

Mix second amount of bread crumbs with paprika in third small bowl.

Melt margarine in frying pan. Coat chicken patties with flour, dip in egg wash, then in crumb-paprika mixture. Brown both sides and cook until no pink remains in meat. After browning, pan may be covered and cooking continued on lower heat, about 20 minutes total time. Makes 9 patties.

PAN GRAVY

Butter or hard margarine	3 tbsp.	50 mL
All-purpose flour	3 tbsp.	50 mL
Salt	1/2 tsp.	2 mL
Pepper	1/8 tsp.	0.5 mL
Water (or milk)	1 1/2 cups	350 mL

Stir butter in frying pan to melt. Add flour, salt and pepper. Mix.

Stir in water, loosening all brown bits, until it boils and thickens. Makes 1 1/2 cups (350 mL).

ALFREDO SAUCED CHICKEN

A great meal. Full of noodles, chicken and peas in a honey-garlic sauce.

Cooking oil	2 tbsp.	30 mL
Small boneless chicken breast halves, skin removed, cut in short narrow strips	6	6
Fettuccine	1 lb.	500 g
Boiling water	4 qts.	4 L
Cooking oil	1 tbsp.	15 mL
Salt	1 tbsp.	15 mL
Butter or hard margarine	½ cup	125 mL
Whipping cream	1 cup	250 mL
Honey	¼ cup	60 mL
White wine (or alcohol-free wine)	¼ cup	60 mL
Garlic powder	¼ tsp.	1 mL
Frozen peas	1 cup	250 mL
Grated Parmesan cheese	½ cup	125 mL
Parsley flakes	1 tsp.	5 mL
Salt	1 tsp.	5 mL
Pepper	¼ tsp.	1 mL

Heat cooking oil in frying pan. Add chicken. Sauté for about 5 minutes until no pink remains.

Cook fettuccine in boiling water, cooking oil and salt in large uncovered pot for 5 to 7 minutes until tender but firm. Drain. Return noodles to pot.

Add next 6 ingredients to chicken. Heat and stir until it simmers. Stir into pasta in pot.

Add remaining ingredients to pasta. Toss to mix well. Makes generous 12 cups (2.7 L) to serve 6.

Confucius say "Never see catfish but see horsefly."

CHICKEN DUMPLINGS

The dark economical meat works well in this.

Boneless chicken, skin removed	1½ lbs.	680 g
Butter or hard margarine	2 tbsp.	30 mL
Salt	1 tsp.	5 mL
Pepper	¼ tsp.	1 mL
Water	3 cups	700 mL
Finely chopped onion	⅓ cup	75 mL
Finely chopped celery	3 tbsp.	50 mL
Chicken bouillon powder	1 tsp.	5 mL
DUMPLINGS		
All-purpose flour	1 cup	250 mL
Baking powder	2 tsp.	10 mL
Granulated sugar	1 tsp.	5 mL
Salt	½ tsp.	2 mL
Cold butter or hard margarine	1 tbsp.	15 mL
Milk	½ cup	125 mL
All-purpose flour	3 tbsp.	50 mL
Water	⅓ cup	75 mL

Cut chicken into bite size pieces. Heat first amount of butter in frying pan. Add chicken. Brown well over medium-high heat. Turn into large saucepan.

Add salt and pepper to frying pan. Stir in water until it boils. Loosen all brown bits. Pour over chicken.

Add onion, celery and bouillon powder. If any pink is still in meat, cover and simmer until cooked.

Dumplings: Measure first amount of flour, baking powder, sugar and salt into bowl. Cut in butter until mealy. Add milk. Stir to form a dough. Have chicken mixture boiling. Drop dough by 6 or more spoonfuls over top. Cover. Cook over boiling mixture for 15 minutes without lifting lid. Remove dumplings to plate.

Mix remaining flour and water in small dish until smooth. Stir into boiling mixture to thicken. Serves 6.

METRIC CONVERSION

Throughout this book measurements are given in Conventional and Metric measure. To compensate for differences between the two measurements due to rounding, a full metric measure is not always used. The cup used is the standard 8 fluid ounce. Temperature is given in degrees Fahrenheit and Celsius. Baking pan measurements are in inches and centimetres as well as quarts and litres. An exact metric conversion is given below as well as the working equivalent (Standard Measure).

OVEN TEMPERATURES

Fahrenheit (°F)	Celsius (°C)
175°	80°
200°	95°
225°	110°
250°	120°
275°	140°
300°	150°
325°	160°
350°	175°
375°	190°
400°	205°
425°	220°
450°	230°
475°	240°
500°	260°

SPOONS

Conventional Measure	Metric Exact Conversion Millilitre (mL)	Metric Standard Measure Millilitre (mL)
1/4 teaspoon (tsp.)	1.2 mL	1 mL
1/2 teaspoon (tsp.)	2.4 mL	2 mL
1 teaspoon (tsp.)	4.7 mL	5 mL
2 teaspoons (tsp.)	9.4 mL	10 mL
1 tablespoon (tbsp.)	14.2 mL	15 mL

CUPS

Conventional Measure	Metric Exact Conversion	Metric Standard Measure
1/4 cup (4 tbsp.)	56.8 mL	50 mL
1/3 cup (5 1/3 tbsp.)	75.6 mL	75 mL
1/2 cup (8 tbsp.)	113.7 mL	125 mL
2/3 cup (10 2/3 tbsp.)	151.2 mL	150 mL
3/4 cup (12 tbsp.)	170.5 mL	175 mL
1 cup (16 tbsp.)	227.3 mL	250 mL
4 1/2 cups	1022.9 mL	1000 mL (1 L)

DRY MEASUREMENTS

Ounces (oz.)	Grams (g)	Grams (g)
1 oz.	28.3 g	30 g
2 oz.	56.7 g	55 g
3 oz.	85.0 g	85 g
4 oz.	113.4 g	125 g
5 oz.	141.7 g	140 g
6 oz.	170.1 g	170 g
7 oz.	198.4 g	200 g
8 oz.	226.8 g	250 g
16 oz.	453.6 g	500 g
32 oz.	907.2 g	1000 g (1 kg)

PANS, CASSEROLES

Conventional Inches	Metric Centimetres	Conventional Quart (qt.)	Metric Litre (L)
8x8 inch	20x20 cm	1 2/3 qt.	2 L
9x9 inch	22x22 cm	2 qt.	2.5 L
9x13 inch	22x33 cm	3 1/3 qt.	4 L
10x15 inch	25x38 cm	1 qt.	1.2 L
11x17 inch	28x43 cm	1 1/4 qt.	1.5 L
8x2 inch round	20x5 cm	1 2/3 qt.	2 L
9x2 inch round	22x5 cm	2 qt.	2.5 L
10x4 1/2 inch tube	25x11 cm	4 1/4 qt.	5 L
8x4x3 inch loaf	20x10x7 cm	1 1/4 qt.	1.5 L
9x5x3 inch loaf	23x12x7 cm	1 2/3 qt.	2 L

INDEX

MAIL ORDER COUPON
Save $5.00!
Deduct $5.00 for every $35.00 ordered

QUANTITY • HARD COVER BOOK

[ ] Jean Paré's Favorites - Volume One

$17.95 + $1.50 shipping = **$19.45 each** x [ ]

NO. OF BOOKS | PRICE
= $ [ ]

ENGLISH

QUANTITY • SOFT COVER BOOKS

[ ] 150 Delicious Squares	[ ] Cakes
[ ] Casseroles	[ ] Barbecues
[ ] Muffins & More	[ ] Dinners of the World
[ ] Salads	[ ] Lunches
[ ] Appetizers	[ ] Pies
[ ] Desserts	[ ] Light Recipes
[ ] Soups & Sandwiches	[ ] Microwave Cooking
[ ] Holiday Entertaining	[ ] Preserves
[ ] Cookies	[ ] Light Casseroles
[ ] Vegetables	[ ] Chicken, Etc.
[ ] Main Courses	NEW [ ] Kids Cooking (August '95)
[ ] Pasta	

NO. OF BOOKS | PRICE

$10.95 + $1.50 shipping = **$12.45 each** x [ ] = $ [ ]

QUANTITY • PINT SIZE BOOKS (SOFT COVER)

| [ ] Finger Food | [ ] Buffets |
| [ ] Party Planning | NEW [ ] Baking Delights |

NO. OF BOOKS | PRICE

$4.99 + $1.00 shipping = **$5.99 each** x [ ] = $ [ ]

FRENCH

QUANTITY • SOFT COVER BOOKS

[ ] 150 délicieux carrés	[ ] Les salades
[ ] Les casseroles	[ ] La cuisson au micro-ondes
[ ] Muffins et plus	[ ] Les pâtes
[ ] Les dîners	[ ] Les conserves
[ ] Les barbecues	[ ] Les casseroles légères
[ ] Les tartes	[ ] Poulet, etc.
[ ] Délices des fêtes	NEW [ ] La cuisine pour les enfants (août '95)
[ ] Recettes légères	

NO. OF BOOKS | PRICE

$10.95 + $1.50 shipping = **$12.45 each** x [ ] = $ [ ]

TOTAL

- **MAKE CHEQUE OR MONEY ORDER PAYABLE TO:** *COMPANY'S COMING PUBLISHING LIMITED*

- **ORDERS OUTSIDE CANADA:** *Must be paid in U.S. funds by cheque or money order drawn on Canadian or U.S. bank.*

- *Prices subject to change without prior notice.*

- *Sorry, no C.O.D.'s*

TOTAL PRICE FOR ALL BOOKS	$
Less $5.00 for every $35.00 ordered −	$
SUBTOTAL	$
Canadian residents add G.S.T. +	$
TOTAL AMOUNT ENCLOSED	$

Please complete shipping address on reverse.

Gift Giving

- Let us help you with your gift giving!

- We will send cookbooks directly to the recipients of your choice if you give us their names and addresses.

- Be sure to specify the titles you wish to send to each person.

- If you would like to include your personal note or card, we will be pleased to enclose it with your gift order.

- Company's Coming Cookbooks make excellent gifts. Birthdays, bridal showers, Mother's Day, Father's Day, graduation or any occasion... collect them all!

Shipping address

Send the Company's Coming Cookbooks listed on the reverse side of this coupon, to:

Name:

Street:

City: Province/State:

Postal Code/Zip: Tel: (   )   —

COOKBOOKS

Company's Coming Publishing Limited
Box 8037, Station F
Edmonton, Alberta, Canada T6H 4N9
Tel: (403) 450-6223

Sample Recipe from
Kids Cooking

Crispy Fruit Pizza

A dessert pizza you can eat with your fingers. Can be made the day before. This is AWESOME!

1. CRUST

Butter or hard margarine	¼ cup	60 mL
Large marshmallows	32	32

2. Crisp rice cereal — 5 cups — 1.25 L

3. TOPPING

Cream cheese, softened	8 oz.	250 g
Icing (confectioner's) sugar	2 cups	500 mL
Cocoa	¼ cup	60 mL

4.

Small strawberries, halved, reserve 1 whole berry	16	16
Banana, peeled and sliced	1	1
Kiwifruit, peeled, halved lengthwise and sliced	2	2

5. GLAZE

Apricot jam	2 tbsp.	30 mL
Water	1½ tsp.	7 mL

6.

Whipping cream (or 1 envelope topping)	1 cup	250 mL
Granulated sugar	2 tsp.	10 mL
Vanilla flavoring	½ tsp.	2 mL

You will need: a large saucepan, measuring spoons, measuring cups, 3 mixing spoons, a hot pad, a 12 inch (30 cm) pizza pan, a small bowl, an electric beater, a small cup, a pastry brush and a medium bowl.

1. Crust: Combine the butter or margarine and marshmallows in the saucepan. Stir continually on medium-low heat until melted.

2. Remove the saucepan to the hot pad. Add the rice cereal. Stir until it is well coated. Grease the pizza pan. Press the cereal mixture evenly over the pan with your wet fingers. Cool in the refrigerator.

3. Topping: Place the cream cheese, icing sugar and cocoa in the small bowl. Beat on low speed until moistened. Beat on medium speed until smooth. Spread over the cooled pizza base.

4. Arrange the strawberries, bananas and kiwifruit over the chocolate topping in a fancy design.

5. Glaze: Mix the jam and water in the cup. With the pastry brush, dab the fruit with the jam mixture to glaze and to prevent the fruit from turning brown.

6. Beat the whipping cream, sugar and vanilla in the medium bowl until thick. Put dabs on top of pizza. Cut into 8 or 10 wedges.

Use this handy checklist to
complete your collection of
Company's Coming Cookbooks